DBT Metaphors and Stories

DBT Metaphors and Stories gives therapists and DBT skills trainers the skills they need to make effective use of dialectical behavior therapy and to help clients more deeply understand complex realities.

Each page is devoted to explaining a specific DBT skill. The book is structured so that it can be used in several ways, including as a reference tool to look up specific skills the reader is struggling to understand or (for skills trainers) to teach. The book can also be read cover to cover, both for understanding the broad array of skills and as a source of motivation to devote one's self to regular practice of skills. It's a vital guide for trainers, therapists, and their clients interested in fully harnessing DBT's power to change lives.

James J. Esmail, PsyD, is a clinical psychologist at Summit Behavioral Healthcare and in private practice, and he is also an adjunct professor in the graduate school of psychology at Xavier University.

DBT Metaphors and Stories

Understanding the Skills that Make Life Worth Living

James J. Esmail

Routledge
Taylor & Francis Group

NEW YORK AND LONDON

First published 2021
by Routledge
52 Vanderbilt Avenue, New York, NY 10017

and by Routledge
2 Park Square, Milton Park, Abingdon, Oxon OX14 4RN

Routledge is an imprint of the Taylor & Francis Group, an informa business

Library of Congress Cataloging-in-Publication Data
A catalog record for this title has been requested

ISBN: 978-0-367-63623-4 (hbk)
ISBN: 978-0-367-63621-0 (pbk)
ISBN: 978-1-003-12511-2 (ebk)

Typeset in Calvert
by Newgen Publishing UK

Contents

Preface

This volume is intended for persons in DBT skills training who want to think more deeply about DBT skills and DBT concepts that they are learning about and practicing, as well as for DBT skills trainers who are looking for metaphors to explain the DBT skills. This book is not intended as a replacement for being in a DBT skills training group with a qualified mental health professional, nor is it a substitute for the DBT Skills Training Handouts and Worksheets (2015) by Marsha Linehan, PhD.

Thinking in metaphors is one of the crucial building blocks that allows humans to engage in abstract reasoning. The ability to compare something that is abstract and difficult to something more concrete and tangible is what has allowed humans to go beyond very simple cognition (Landau, Robinson, and Meier, 2014) to understanding the more complex realities in life.

Marsha Linehan notes: "... the use of metaphor, in the form of simple analogies, antidotes, parables, myths or stories, is extremely important in DBT. Metaphors are an alternative means of teaching dialectical thinking and opening up possibilities of new behaviors" (Linehan, 1993, p. 209). Linehan points to Milton Erickson, a master of storytelling, to affect therapeutic change.

> Metaphors and stories have been used throughout history to convey complex events that can have multiple meanings. Stories are also an avenue of clarifying what a person is leaving out in his or her understanding of something. For example, a person may be focused on not wanting to come to the skills training group and decide that the skills are not needed to achieve his or her goals. You can point out that this is like getting in a boat to go across the river when the boat has no bottom in it. Trying to be what others want a person to be like is a tulip trying to be a rose just because it happens to have been planted in the Rose Garden.
>
> (Linehan, 1993, p. 209)

Likewise, Aaron Beck and his colleagues (2015) note that therapy should be imbued with "a sense of adventure," otherwise "therapy can decline into a repetitive process that becomes increasingly tedious over time" (p. 107). Beck says the solution is the use of "metaphors and anecdotes" as well as "a certain lightness and judicious use of humor" to add spice to the therapy experience. I trust you will find this volume to be full of metaphors, anecdotes, and humor, and that it will spice up your experience of DBT.

The metaphors, stories, and meditations in this book are simply ones that I have created over the last 14 years teaching DBT skills both at the state psychiatric hospital in Cincinnati and in my private practice. Through the years, a number of people have told me these metaphors were useful in helping them to grasp DBT skills, and suggested that I compile them into a book to share them beyond the groups I lead.

Two things about this book are important to note. First, you can read it one page at a time. Each page is devoted to explaining a specific DBT skill, and is a self-contained explanation of the skill. If you are in a DBT skills group and want to understand more about Opposite Action or Improve the Moment with Vacation, just flip to the appropriate page. Using the book this way does not require you to start at the beginning of the book and work forward. The book is structured this way so you can use is as a reference tool to look up specific skills you are working on understanding and mastering. Second, the book is designed not just to explain the skills, but to motivate you to practice and use them. Knowing how to solve a problem is only half the battle. The other half is to be motivated to put the skills into action. It is my hope that you will draw much inspiration from this book, inspiration that will move you to devote yourself to the study and practice of the skills on a regular basis. It is one thing to receive a guitar lesson, it is another to put in the time to practice. Hopefully what you read will excite you into action.

A word of thanks goes to a number of persons. First and foremost, Desirae Allen, PsyD who read the original manuscript and provided technical as well as stylistic advice and assistance for this project. Desirae was crucial in helping me with many of the technical aspects of writing such a book, including organizing the material into a form that was easily accessible. Desirae is also a skillful psychologist who is deeply committed to teaching and modeling DBT skills.

Secondly, Nick Salsman, PhD, professor of psychology at Xavier University, has provided tremendous help in a number of ways. Nick has done research with Marsha Linehan, trained with her, and has co-led a DBT skills group with her. When Nick came to Cincinnati, he generously volunteered his time to teach many of us at the state hospital as well as clinicians in private practice about DBT skills training. Nick also generously reviewed this manuscript and contributed valuable suggestions.

I would also like to thank the number of people who have been my co-therapists in DBT skills training groups. This group includes Rena Mei-Tal, PsyD, ABPP, Diane Shufford, M.ORT, M. Ed, Lauren Feria, PsyD, Bailey Bryant, PsyD, Nikki Winchester, PsyD, and Desirae Allen, PsyD. Many thanks also to the many graduate students who helped lead DBT skills groups with me at the state hospital.

Thanks to my editor at Routledge, Anna Moore, who gave my book a chance and provided valuable guidance throughout the process of getting this work published. Thanks to Geof Yaeger, PhD, Rena Mei-Tal, PsyD, ABPP, Karl Stukenberg, PhD, ABPP, and Brett Dowdy, PsyD for reviewing the manuscript and critiquing the contents. Your contribution is greatly appreciated.

Lastly, I want to thank my wife and two teenage sons. You have taught me the value of being mindful in a way that exceeds anything I could learn from a book.

REFERENCES

Beck, A T, Davis, D D, & Freeman, A. (2015) *Cognitive therapy of personality disorders*, 3rd Edition. New York: Guilford.

Landau, M J, Robinson, M D, & Meier, B P. (2014) *The power of metaphor: Examining its influence on social life*. Washington, D.C.: American Psychological Association.

Linehan, M M. (1993) *Cognitive-behavioral treatment of borderline personality disorder*. New York: Guilford.

Linehan, M M. (2015) *DBT skills training: Handouts and worksheets*. New York: Guilford.

About the Author

James J. Esmail, PsyD is a clinical psychologist who has been in practice since 1996. He earned his MA and PsyD degrees in clinical psychology from Spalding University in Louisville, Kentucky. Dr Esmail is a staff psychologist at the state psychiatric hospital in Cincinnati, Ohio (Summit Behavioral Healthcare), is in private practice, and is an adjunct professor in the Doctor of Psychology program at Xavier University.

Dr Esmail has led DBT groups at both the state hospital and in his private practice for the last 12 years. He has enjoyed seeing DBT change the lives of the patients he works with, but also recognizes how DBT has enhanced both his life and the lives of his group co-leaders, many of whom have been clinical psychology doctoral candidates from the University of Cincinnati, Xavier University, Wright State University, and Miami University.

Aside from his practice, supervision, and teaching responsibilities, Dr Esmail finds many things that make his life worth living. First and foremost are his wife Lynn and teenage sons Noah and Nate, and he also loves playing the guitar, bicycling, reading, doing volunteer work, walking, and exercise.

Why Engage in Skills Training?

Chapter 1

WHY ENGAGE IN SKILLS TRAINING?

METAPHOR—BATMAN

I grew up in the 1960s. In 1966, when I was in the second grade, a TV show came on that rocked my world and the world of my classmates—*Batman* (starring Adam West and Burt Ward; Dozier, 1966).

Each episode, a villain would put Batman and Robin in some dangerous situation, but Batman would reach into his "utility belt" for the perfect weapon or defense to counter what the villain had done. I remember one episode in which Batman and Robin were stung by scorpions, but Batman was able to reach into his utility belt for his "Bat-anti-scorpion-venom antidote."

Your life has been wrought with heartache, emotional pain, relationship failures, and self-destructive behaviors. Your life has been this difficult, in large part, because nobody has given you the complete array of skills needed to cope with life's demands and difficulties. In essence, you are like Batman without a utility belt.

DBT skills training is the answer to this dilemma. You will fill your utility belt with Emotion Regulation, Interpersonal

Effectiveness, and Distress Tolerance skills that will enable you to (in the words of Marsha Linehan) build a life worth living. Mindfulness skills (Linehan, 2015, p. 49) will be the foundation upon which you build the other skills.

It is important to remember that Batman not only had a utility belt filled with tools, but he had honed a great deal of skill in using them by repeated **practice.** For example he had a boomerang (shaped like a bat) which he attached to the "bat-rope": Batman could throw the "Bat-o-rang" with great skill and use it to climb a building or catch a criminal. Just having the "bat-o-rang" was not enough: similarly, you need not only to know about the skills, but acquire skill by practicing them

Dr Linehan recommends that a person engage in a skills training group for at least one year. In my practice, I have noticed that the longer people are in skills training, the more effective they become in using what is in their utility belts. Don't become discouraged if you don't notice a huge difference in your life the first several weeks; stocking your utility belt will take some time. Once it is filled, you will wonder how you made it through life without these tools.

PRACTICING SKILLS—THE IMPORTANCE OF PRACTICE

Some people look at psychotherapy as if it were a modern car wash. You drive up, put your car in neutral, and let the car wash pull your vehicle through—the car wash itself does all the work. You emerge on the other side of the psychotherapy process fully cleansed of your problems. All you must do is pay for the car wash.

DBT is very different than a car wash. One gets the maximum benefit of DBT by doing the homework every week and practicing the skills daily.

Here is one of my early experiences with practice. When I was in fifth grade, I decided to join my school band. The other students all got shiny new instruments, whereas I had to wait a couple weeks to borrow a tarnished old trombone from my cousin Mark. In hindsight, I realize my band teacher felt sorry for me with the tarnished old instrument, and he lavished a lot of encouragement upon me. As such, I practiced regularly and dutifully, and within several months became the best instrumentalist in the whole band. About this time, my parents did buy me a shiny new trombone. The band director began to focus his encouragement and teaching on other students who were struggling to make progress. Without his attention and encouragement, I quit practicing regularly. By the end of the year I diminished to being an average player. Within a couple years, I became one of the worst players in the band, all because I was no longer practicing.

Here is another personal story with a better ending. Unlike probably any other author you have read, I held a part-time job for 30 years at a major shipping company loading trucks. I did this all during college and graduate school, as well as in my early years as a psychologist to supplement my income. I will not tell you which company it was, but I will say our trucks were painted brown. After 28 years of loading, I needed a knee operation. My surgeon explained before the operation the type of exercises he wanted me to do to post-operatively to rehab my knee. I realized my 30-year pension was hanging in the balance, and I did the exercises religiously. I saw the surgeon two weeks after the operation, and he was amazed at my knee's strength and flexibility. He had never seen someone progress so rapidly and completely. Then he told me about the knee exercises again as if I had never heard of them. I said, "oh no, I've been doing this all along." The surgeon expressed amazement that I paid attention to what he said before the operation, and that I actually practiced the exercises. Please note this disclaimer: my diligence in practicing the exercises was not due to my personal virtue, but rather the realization that my 30-year pension (a lot of money) was hanging in the balance. Regular practice makes a huge difference.

How much do you want to get out of your DBT skills group? Invest in your practice accordingly.

WHY STUDY SKILLS—THE KARATE KID

The Karate Kid (Louis & Avildsen, 1984) is a movie about a teenager, Daniel, played by Ralph Macchio, who is bullied by a gang of other teenage boys who are being trained in a renegade form of karate called Cobra Kai. Cobra Kai was considered unethical and vicious by other karate practitioners. When Daniel is being bullied and beaten by five Cobra Kai teens, the maintenance man from his apartment complex, an old man from Okinawa, Mr. Miyagi, intervenes, fighting and beating the five Cobra Kai thugs.

Eventually Mr. Miyagi agrees to teach Daniel karate, but first puts him to work waxing his vintage automobiles. Miyagi teaches Daniel to "wax on" with one arm and "wax off" with the other in a circular motion. After a long period of this, Daniel feels that he is being exploited and angrily protests. At this point, his teacher throws several punches at Daniel, and Daniel blocks these with ease using the same circular motion, thus discovering that what he really was doing was practicing defensive blocks, committing them to muscle memory by repeating the "wax on-wax off" motions. He does not have to think to use the blocks, rather he does them instantly and automatically, without thought.

A hallmark of DBT is practice, practice, practice. You may get tired of doing the homework every week. You may be tempted to not practice the skills on a regular basis. Life can be a very difficult battle, and if you learn the skills to the point that they become second nature, you will be masterful in the ability to defend yourself in the face of life's challenges.

Don't let the repetition of skills practice deter you. The only way to become a master in athletics, playing a musical instrument, or using DBT skills is by repeated practice.

WHY LEARN SKILLS—PARABLE OF TWO LUMBERJACKS

Imagine two lumberjacks living side-by-side. Their boss approaches them one morning, telling them that he needs ten oak trees cut down immediately, and so he is going to give a bonus of $100 to the one who first cuts down ten oaks. Once they finish with the ten trees, they can take the rest of the day off with pay. Remember, oak trees are very hard, and very difficult to cut.

Both lumberjacks are very motivated by this prize, but they approach the challenge very differently. The first lumberjack races out into the woods and begins chopping vigorously at these very hard trees. The second does not go immediately into the woods, in fact there is a half hour delay before he takes his first swing. The second lumberjack spends approximately 30 minutes sharpening his ax. As a result, he soon passes the first lumberjack, who is still vigorously chopping, but with less results.

I have no doubt that you have worked very hard to construct a good life for yourself. Even though you have chopped to the point of blood, sweat, and tears, doing your best, you have not reaped the reward you have sought. Your Wise Mind has told you there has to be a more effective way; hence you have pursued learning DBT skills, including reading this book. Learning the skills that Marsha Linehan has brought together in dialectical behavior therapy is like sharpening your ax. Like the oak trees, life is hard. Learning DBT will not make life easy, but it will make life much **easier** in the long run. Compared to chopping away with the dull ax, using the sharp ax of DBT will be easier.

Bravo to you for having the wisdom to sharpen your ax!

WHY PRACTICE SKILLS—BATTING PRACTICE

If you go to a Major League Baseball game, you will have the opportunity to enter the ballpark early, perhaps as early as two hours before the first inning. Teams allow fans to do this to watch batting practice, with each player taking maybe ten minutes of pitches, practicing their timing, stroke, and body mechanics in preparation for the game.

If you should live close enough to a Major League team to do this, realize what you're looking at. These are not little league players, nor high school athletes. These are not collegiate players or persons in Single A, Double A, or Triple A baseball. Even at the Little League level, you will see a fair amount of skill. In high school and college baseball you will see a lot of skill. When you enter the minor leagues, the skill level is extraordinary, probably everybody on the field was the best player at of about 1000+.

When you watch Major League Baseball, you're watching the best of the best of the best. And yet two hours before game, what are these guys doing? They are taking batting **practice.**

Getting DBT skills to attain tangible benefits in your life does not come by wishing, but by practicing. I don't know about you, but I sure as heck am NOT going to skip batting practice.

WHY PRACTICE SKILLS—THE PARABLE OF THE SLOPPY GUITARIST

I play in a rock and roll band, and we had a very successful gig three nights ago. The other three instrumentalists and our two lead singers sounded really great; people were up dancing and singing along with the songs that we covered.

I, however, did not play so well. I hit some wrong notes, and my timing was not "spot on." I am fortunate that the other five were playing so well that they carried the day.

Why was my guitar playing so sub-par? For the last three to four months I have been working very hard to complete this book (a lifelong ambition). To find time for it, I sacrificed in other areas, and perhaps the area for which I "robbed Peter to pay Paul" was sacrificing guitar practice to write the book. By not practicing, not only was I not getting better, but my skills started to diminish. I remember having a conversation with my long-time guitar teacher, Craig Wilson about this. Both of us agreed that if we did not practice, our skills and execution would begin to erode within days.

The same is true of DBT skills. It is not enough to learn them. We must keep them sharp by practicing on an ongoing basis. Rather than seeing this is some sort of burden, I see it as similar to practicing the guitar. Sometimes there are frustrating exercises that are not easy to implement or rehearse, but most of the time I enjoy practicing, and the benefit manifests itself in a short period of time.

How much will DBT skills pay off in your effort to build a life worth living? Depends on how much you ***practice***.

REFERENCES

Dozier, W (Executive Producer). (1966) *Batman* [Television Series]. United States: 20th Century Fox Television and Greenway Productions.

Linehan, M M. (2015) DBT skills training: Handouts and worksheets. New York: Guilford.

Louis, R J (Executive Producer) & Avildsen, J G (Director). (1984). *The Karate Kid* [Motion Picture]. United States: Columbia Pictures Corporation and Delphi II Productions.

Mindfulness

Chapter 2

MINDFULNESS DEFINITION—*WHAT'S GOING ON*—ALBUM BY MARVIN GAYE

When I explain what Mindfulness is, I often think of the title of Marvin Gaye's classic album, *What's Going On* (Cleveland, Benson, Gaye, 1971). Gaye wrote the album from the vantage point of a solder returning from Viet Nam, observing what and how American was different since his return. Mindfulness is "what's going on." Mindfulness is paying attention to what is going on in your external and internal environments.

Notice what the title is not: it is not "What Went On" or "What Will Go On." Mindfulness is in the present. This does not mean we never think about the past, but when we do, we recognize we are experiencing a memory, not a present reality.

We as humans have the unique ability to think about the past and the future. This ability also poses a potential trap for suffering. Do you ever worry about the future to the point that you feel tortured? Realize that neither a dog, horse, nor giraffe has this same kind of suffering. Hypothesizing about the future can be a useful tool, but it can also be a tyrannical master. Mindfulness practice is about gently bringing our awareness and focus back to the present, to "what's going on" in this very moment.

We will discuss this deliberate steering of our attention to the here-and-now under the *Participate* skill.

By the way, in its list of the 500 Greatest Albums of All Time, *Rolling Stone* ranked *What's Going On* as the sixth greatest album of all time. I hope being present with **what's going on** will be one of the greatest skills you acquire from DBT.

WHAT IS MINDFULNESS? AWARENESS

When I introduce the concept of mindfulness, some people are wary because they fear mindfulness could be some esoteric, supernatural, or religious practice that would clash with their religious convictions or personal comfort level. Mindfulness practice did evolve in the context of Buddhism, as well as some Christian and Islamic traditions (see Thomas Lynch, *Radically Open Dialectical Behavior Therapy*, 2018 for application of mindfulness practice derived from the latter). For Marsha Linehan, as well as other respected psychologists (Jon Kabat-Zinn and Mark Teasdale) mindfulness is neither devoted to nor in opposition to any religious teaching. Mindfulness is simply the **practice of being aware**. Ron Siegel in *The Mindfulness Solution* (2010) defines mindfulness as "awareness + compassion." If your religion is against either awareness or compassion, you have a problem, but I doubt that is the case.

MINDFULNESS OVERVIEW—THIS COULD BE THE "CLIFF'S NOTES" FOR MINDFULNESS

When I was in college, I discovered something that I found very useful—Cliff's Notes. Cliff's Notes are brief summaries of great works of literature, giving an overview of epic tomes. I found that reading the Cliff's Notes first, before reading the work itself, helped me to get an overview of the story. This prevented me getting entirely lost when reading a classic of literature that was written in the 1600s, 1700s, or 1800s, when the English language was very different than it is now.

Right before I sent the final manuscript of this book to the publisher, I ran into what I think is the best overview, in just one paragraph, of what mindfulness is. And so I share this great overview with you. Notice that it cites the inventor of DBT, Marsha Linehan as well as another pioneer of bringing mindfulness practice to Western society, Jon Kabat-Zinn:

Mindfulness can be described as paying attention in a particular way: on purpose, in the present moment and nonjudgmentally (Kabat-Zinn, 1994, p. 3). It can involve a focusing of attention and an acceptance of present moment experiences (Linehan, 1993), as contrasted with cognitive processes such as rumination, worry, planning, and automatic engagement with activity without awareness.

(Morris, Johns, & Oliver, 2013, p. 7)

To further help you grasp the main components of mindfulness in this paragraph, I have broken it down into bullet points. Mindfulness is:

- Paying attention
- Paying attention on purpose
- Paying attention in the present moment
- Paying attention nonjudgmentally
- Focusing your attention
- Accepting the experience of the present moment

The definition continues by defining mindfulness by the **opposite** of what it is:

- Rumination
- Worry
- Planning
- Automatic engagement in activity without awareness (being on "auto pilot" or proceeding through life like a zombie)

The Cliff's Notes company discourages people from just reading their product as a way of skipping reading the original work. Knowing this definition is a good place to start your study of mindfulness. It can give you an overview of what mindfulness is. But tremendous benefit awaits you as you learn, both intellectually and experientially, how to **practice** mindfulness.

TEFLON MIND—BEST DEPICTION BY A FILM

DBT encourages us to cultivate a "Teflon Mind," which is a great metaphor for allowing ourselves to experience thoughts and feelings, but not letting them "stick" (Linehan, 2015b, pp. 179 & 181). Teflon is the trade name of a synthetic fluoropolymer that is used to create a non-stick surface on cookware. Since the introduction of Teflon, other means of creating stick-free cookware have been introduced, such as cookware that has a titanium surface (some think that use of Teflon in cookware creates health risks, but its use here as a metaphor is entirely free of health risks).

Two useful examples of someone exercising a Teflon Mind are Dan Aykroyd's character, "Boolie" and Morgan Freeman's character "Hoke" in the Academy Award winning movie *Driving Miss Daisy* (Brown & Beresford, 1989). Miss Daisy Werthan is a 72-year-old widow living in Atlanta, Georgia. She is cranky and set in her ways, and in the beginning of the film she is extremely critical and judgmental, including of her 40-year-old son Boolie, and later of the chauffeur that he hires (Hoke). Miss Daisy criticizes her son's choice of a wife, their celebrating of Christmas (she is Jewish), and the many practical things he does for her. Throughout the film, Boolie shakes off his mother's criticism and agitation, choosing to not take it too personally. Likewise, Hoke side-steps Miss Daisy's criticism, rejection, and nastiness. Hoke's Teflon mind allows him to treat Miss Daisy with respect and dignity. Over the long haul, these Teflon minds influence Miss Daisy to let go of her judgmental attitude and hyper-critical behavior. By the end of the movie, Miss Daisy has been transformed from a bitter and stubborn woman to a gentle and caring senior.

I invite you to watch the film and observe how skillfully both Hoke and Boolie use Teflon Mind to reduce what otherwise would cause tremendous wear and tear on their psyches. Teflon Mind minimizes the effect of Miss Daisy's harsh, critical rhetoric. These harsh critical statements just don't "stick." This frees them up to do what is most effective on Miss Daisy's behalf.

Driving Miss Daisy (Brown & Beresford, 1989) won four Academy Awards, including for Best Picture and Best Actress. Morgan Freeman and Dan Aykroyd also received Academy

Award nominations for Best Actor and Best Supporting Actor. It is a good film to watch. I wish I could nominate it for another Academy Award, a new category which I would entitle **Best Film Depicting a DBT Skill**, which in this case would be for its depiction of **Teflon Mind**.

MINDFULNESS RIDDLE—HOW MANY SIDES DOES A BASKETBALL HAVE?

In my DBT skills groups I pose the question, "How many sides does a basketball have?" Various people have various reactions. Some think this is a trick question and say, "It has no sides, it's a ball!" Others think of the round surface and say it has just one side that is continuous.

I then give them my answer: a basketball has two sides. Most people are perplexed by this until I explain, "The basketball has two sides, **the** *inside* and **the** *outside*."

Mindfulness practice has the same two sides. You will practice Observing and Describing what goes on inside of you: your emotions, thoughts, bodily sensations, etc. Likewise, you will develop your skill at Observing and Describing what is outside of you: your physical and social environment.

Most people do not realize how little they pay attention to what is going on inside them. They know some of what is on the inside, but I have discovered that many people are only aware of fragments of the whole picture. I continue to be amazed when I ask, "What are you feeling right now?" They will reply with all sorts of answers, but few respond to my question about the emotion they are experiencing in the moment. I then begin to gently coach them on how to become aware of their emotion and how to describe it. Usually the first step is to help them become aware that they are responding to my inquiry about emotion by responding with a fact, thought, or theory rather than what they are experiencing at an emotional level. I tell them that this is like asking what color their car is, and they respond by saying "It's a Toyota."

As you will learn in the Mindfulness module, to be in what DBT terms "Wise Mind" you have to be in touch with both your intellect and your emotions (some people say "both head and heart"). Without all aspects of your inner world, including emotions, there is no Wise Mind.

It is also fascinating how we can drift through our external world without really being mindful of so much that is there. When people start becoming more aware of their physical and social environment, this simple change starts making a positive difference in their lives. A common example I frequently observe is that a patient in group therapy will be talking about how lonely and alone they are; they see the world as socially barren. Many times these persons are avoiding eye contact with others in the group, and I invite them to look at the facial expressions of fellow group members who, more often than not, are exhibiting concern, compassion, and connectedness.

An early episode of the Simpsons (Brooks, Groening, & Simon, 1989) featured the family playing Scrabble. Homer looks at his set of letters, which spells out "oxidation" and laments "How could anyone make a word out of these lousy letters?!" Homer's problem was not that he didn't have sufficient resources in his environment, but that he didn't have the awareness of what was in his environment. As you become more aware of what is in your environment, you may be surprised to find that a winning combination is right in front of you.

CORE MINDFULNESS—THE IMPORTANCE FOR OTHER SKILL MODULES

When I first began teaching DBT, I did not see much usefulness to the mindfulness material and thought of it as something to breeze through quickly so we could get "to the good stuff" (e.g. Emotion Regulation and Interpersonal Effectiveness). Only when I had been through the curriculum about three times did I begin to grasp that Mindfulness skills, by themselves, have tremendous potential to make positive changes to a person's life. But that's only half the story.

Linehan referred to mindfulness as **core** in the first edition of the manual because it is the foundation on which the other three skill sets are built.

Have you ever seen a skyscraper being built? For months all effort is focused on digging a humongous hole. Next construction workers drill down into the bedrock and secure anchors for the building. The foundation is laid and built up to ground level. To the very casual observer, it may seem that not much is being accomplished in the first two, three, four months. But unless this part is done correctly, the whole building will fall apart. Also, as a general rule, the higher one wants to build, the deeper the foundation will have to be.

The same is true of your Emotion Regulation, Interpersonal Effectiveness, and Distress Tolerance skills. These skills will only work to the degree to which you ground them in mindful awareness. Interpersonal Effectiveness skills will only work to the degree to which you are aware of the actions and facial expressions of people in your social environment. You can practice the Interpersonal Effectiveness skills laid out in the acronyms DEAR MAN, GIVE, and FAST, yet if you are not mindful of the facial expressions, tone of voice, and posture of the people you are relating with, these skills will yield limited results.

Mindfulness skills are also like the root system of a tree. A tree can only grow as large as its root system is able to expand and draw nutrients and water from the soil. You may never see the roots, but without them there would be no trunk, branches, or leaves. Mindfulness skills will be the root system that feeds your Interpersonal Effectiveness, Emotion Regulation, and Distress Tolerance skills.

HOMER SIMPSON—THE PATRON SAINT OF MINDLESSNESS

Often, we best understand something through its opposite. Dry is the opposite of wet. Warm is the opposite of cold. Dark is the opposite of light.

When explaining what mindfulness is, I often point out that the opposite is mind*less*ness, namely doing something with no awareness of what we're doing.

As a college freshman I took a public speaking course. I was very nervous getting up in front of the class and delivering my first speech, which was, as I recall, a five-minute discussion of the United States selling grain to the Soviet Union. I nervously talked to the class for about the required five minutes, and sat down. The first thing the professor said was, "Are you aware that you used the phrase 'you know' a lot?" The whole class chuckled. I replied, "no." Now the class laughed even harder.

I like using Homer Simpson as the patron saint of mindlessness. Homer drives his truck across a rickety bridge, then looks over and sees there is a parallel bridge in good repair. In the Simpsons Movie, he rescues a pig from being butchered at a Krustyburger restaurant, takes it home, and is playing with it like a pet, while neglecting his son Bart. Bart is obviously envious of the pig, who is getting all of Homer's affection. When Homer utters his trademark "D'oh!" it is usually because he has just engaged in another act of mindlessness.

We realize Homer Simpson is often mindless, but we don't judge him. Instead we are fond of him, in spite of his shortcomings, in spite of his mindlessness, maybe even because of his mindlessness. Most of us have a sentiment of loving kindness towards Homer, which makes him the perfect patron saint for mindlessness. At times, we are all mindless. At times, we are Homer. The mindful way to respond to our own mindlessness is not to judge or punish ourselves, but to become aware, and gently, with compassion, bring ourselves back to being aware. Remember that becoming aware that we are not aware is itself an act of mindfulness.

Remember that mindfulness is awareness **plus** compassion (Siegel, 2010).

MINDFULNESS—WHY AWARENESS IS IMPORTANT

Early in my training as a psychologist, my graduate school faculty identified how unaware I was of the emotions of my patients as well as my own emotions. To correct this deficiency, they recommended training in something call Gestalt Therapy and sent me to a three-day training 250 miles from my home at the Gestalt Institute of Cleveland. They hoped this would offset my tendency to be very intellectualized and to ignore the emotions of my clients.

On the first day of training, our instructor drew a circle on the easel board that was labeled "the Cycle of Experience." The beginning point of the circle was labeled "homeostasis— the person at rest," then proceeded through other stages including "need," "sensation of need," "awareness of need," "decision of how to meet need," "action," "contact with the environment to meet the need," "satisfaction/relief," "withdrawal from contact," and finally a return to "homeostasis" or rest. Then the instructor said, "and this is *all* that we are going to study for the next three days."

Man was I pissed! Inside I was fuming and said (to myself), "I drove 250 miles for this?! This is the stupidest" (notice-a judgement on my part) "Mickey Mouse thing I have ever seen!"

And then a funny thing happened. The student next to me raised his hand and said, "Oh, I can see exactly where this is going. I work with alcoholics and drug abusers, and when they get to the part where they have a need, they skip right past awareness to action. Before they're even aware of their need, they switch to auto-pilot and reach for a bottle or drug. They have no awareness of their emotions or their decision to deal with the emotions through the substance." Suddenly, this didn't look so stupid after all.

In DBT you will do the same thing. You will break down your internal process to understand and be aware of your thoughts, emotions, images, decisions, and behaviors, as well as how they are linked together. You will switch from semi-consciously drifting along on autopilot to becoming aware of your whole experience. This will provide you with the opportunity to make better choices at every point in the cycle. Making this change, you will no longer experience your life as being a pre-programmed robot, just going through the motions. Having more awareness, we can avoid making the same mistakes over and over, because we see so much more of the landscape of our lives.

Mindful awareness puts us in control of our lives. No more autopilot.

MINDFULNESS OF YOUR EMOTIONS—READING THE GAUGES IN YOUR COCKPIT

When teaching persons in DBT about the importance of being able to identify our emotions and connect the correct "Describe" label to them, I compare emotions to the cockpit of a plane. The cockpit of an airplane contains many dials and gauges that mean nothing to you or me, but to a pilot these are vital indicators of where the plane is in space, its pitch, altitude, speed, and its relationship to the ground. .

Each of our emotions are like a gauge in our own cockpit. Each emotion tells us something about ourselves and our relationship to our environment. Fear (if it is based in realistic, accurate perception of the situation) tells us there is a danger to avoid. Love tells us we want to spend more time with the object of our love. Guilt tells us that we have harmed someone, to avoid repeating the behavior that triggered the feeling of guilt, and perhaps that we want to make restitution to the injured party. Through the years, pilots who were not trained and certified to fly "instruments only" (in foggy conditions with zero visibility), have crashed and died along with their passengers. One notable example this was John F Kennedy, Jr., son of the 35th president of the United States. Another was a man by the name of Randy Hughes, who was the manager of country music Superstar Patsy Cline. He piloted the single-prop plane in which Cline died when they ran into zero visibility weather.

Awareness of our minute-by-minute emotional experience is essential for being able to build a life worth living. If we can't read our "gauges," if we don't recognize our own feelings, we are, in effect, "flying blind."

MINDFULNESS—BECOMING AWARE OF WHAT YOUR MIND IS DOING—METAPHOR—ROCKY

Mindfulness practice helps us focus our attention where we choose, rather than being at the whim of our mind. It helps us be aware when our mind is running to a place that is not effective for us, such as ruminating about the past or future, rather than being fully present in the present. Mindfulness teachers speak of a condition called "monkey mind" in which our mind chatters incessantly like a monkey, churning out a plethora of thoughts that overwhelm our consciousness. If you have fallen into monkey mind, you probably wish you could just turn off your thought processes and give yourself a break from the incessant chatter.

In the movie *Rocky* (Kirkwood & Avildsen, 1976), veteran boxing coach "Mickey," played by Burgess Meredith, begins to work with Rocky in preparation for the biggest fight of his career. At one point, Rocky is sparring and Mickey calls time out, pointing out that Rocky is very sloppy to the point that it is aggravating Mickey to his wits end. Mickey points out how poor Rocky's footwork is. Rocky is usually off balance, which reduces the power of his punches and also puts him in a position of vulnerability opposite his opponent. Rocky replies he has never had good footwork, so what is the point now? Mickey then ties a string around both ankles about 18 inches apart, telling Rocky if he can box without breaking the string, he will improve his balance and become a very dangerous fighter

The string was a mindfulness tool. It helped Rocky become more aware of what he was doing with his feet. If he began to feel the string, he was at the edge of how far apart his feet should be; the gentle tugging of the string helped him be aware that he was at the outer limits of what would be effective. Rocky moved from boxing in a *mindless* fashion to boxing more *mindfully*.

Mindfulness practice will help you be aware of when your mind is leaving the present to ruminate about the past or worry about the future. This will allow you to gently bring your mind back to the present. Mindfulness practice will help you realize when your mind goes into overdrive or "monkey mind," churning out incessant internal chatter, and will bring your focus back to where *you choose*.

For perhaps the first time in your life, you will no longer be fighting the match of life "off balance."

BECOMING MINDFUL OF WHEN YOU ARE NOT MINDFUL: MRS. PEBBLE

Mindfulness includes being able to direct our mind and focus it where we want it to focus. An important component of mindfulness is realizing when our mind slips away from where we intend it to be.

As a third grader, I was not good at concentrating or staying focused. What I was good at was daydreaming—looking out the window and drifting into a fantasy world where I was a soldier, an astronaut, or a myriad of other things. As such, the percentage of time that I was actually locked in on what was going on in class was not ideal. My teacher was Mrs. Pebble, a kind but pragmatic, no-nonsense woman who was very perceptive. She could observe the look on my face, the look in my eyes, and tell that I was daydreaming. Early in the year she would say, "James, are you focusing on this problem?" or, "James, why don't you read the next sentence?" and I was busted. I didn't even realize that I had drifted away until I heard my name. Later in the year all she would have to say is "James…" and I came back to the reality of the classroom.

Our minds wander, like mine did in third grade. We don't even realize that we are rummaging through our past, fantasizing about our future, living in some fantasy, or completely tuned out of a conversation. But *becoming aware that we are not mindful in that moment is an epiphany of mindfulness*. We are now aware that we are not present in the moment, and that allows us to bring our focus back to where we want it to be. *Becoming mindful that we are not mindful* is a *pivotal shift* back to being mindful.

Thank goodness I had Mrs. Pebble as a teacher in third grade. Thank goodness she still lives in me, calling my name when my mind gets lost in space.

WISE MIND: THE WISE-MINDED PRIMARY CARE PHYSICIAN

In my early forties I had an annual checkup with my primary care physician. I had given some blood the week before for labs, and I went to his office for my annual checkup. I went into the examination room and the first thing that Dr Hellman said was, "Let's get you up on the scale." He then moved the weights over and said, with a little bit of surprise in his voice "252 pounds." His eyebrows raised a little bit.

Next, Dr Hellman had me sit down, and he opened up a manila folder with the results of my labs. I saw his eyes become very wide and he gravely spoke, "Your cholesterol is up … your triglycerides are up … your blood pressure is up … and your weight is up. You are in trouble." A huge wave of fear shot through my body.

Over the next several months, I lost 30 pounds and I have continued to work at dropping my weight below 180 pounds. If Dr Hellman had approached this solely from Reasonable Mind, telling me that my cholesterol, triglycerides, and weight were too high in a matter-of-fact way, I really doubt that I would have become sufficiently motivated to lose the weight because I really do love eating. What Dr Hellman did was combine the factual information from his Reasonable Mind with his genuine Emotion Mind **fear** (he really did care for me). By doing this, he conveyed to me his concern in a very Wise-Minded manner. Reasonable Mind without Emotion Mind (or Emotion Mind without Reasonable Mind) is not nearly as effective as both working together. Both are needed to be in Wise Mind.

I have no doubt that it took the Wise Minded communication from my doctor to save my life.

WISE MIND—EVERYBODY HAS IT

When we are first taught about Wise Mind, we may feel discouraged. Due to having lived in Emotion Mind much of the time, we can feel we may never attain Wise Mind. Marsha Linehan points out we all have Wise Mind, and she invites us to think back to a time where we knew the right thing intellectually, and also felt that it was right in our "gut." We accessed wisdom and made a good choice.

The film The Wizard of Oz (Fleming, 1939) depicts the heroine, Dorothy, whisked out of her native Kansas by a tornado and deposited in the strange land of Oz. Dorothy meets new friends in her pilgrimage to seek the help of the Wizard. First she meets the Scarecrow, a friendly and kind soul who laments, "If I only had a brain." They then meet the Tinman on the road, a strong and trustworthy person who laments, "If I only had a heart." Lastly they meet the Cowardly Lion, who wishes he had courage. When they meet the Wizard, he angrily chastises them for daring to ask for what they want (a return trip to Kansas, a brain, a heart, and courage). Nonetheless, the Wizard drives a hard bargain: they must first capture the broom of the Wicked Witch of the West, then he *might* consider their requests.

The quartet embarks to obtain (by theft) the Wicked Witch's broom, and are beset with many hazards (such as those horrible flying monkeys). The Witch's troops have Dorothy and her gang pinned down, and the Witch grabs a torch to sadistically burn the Scarecrow. Dorothy comes to his aid by throwing a bucket of water to douse the flames on Scarecrow. Part of the water hits the Witch, and her weakness is revealed: water causes her to melt.

The quartet returns to the Wizard, who is pleased that they have secured the broom (and killed the Witch), but now he is stonewalling on granting them their wishes. The Wizard is exposed as not some mighty being, but just a normal man, trying to help the people of Oz.

When Dorothy rebukes the Wizard for not having the power to grant their wishes, the Wizard points out some surprising truths. The Scarecrow demonstrated tremendous ingenuity in their quest to penetrate the Witch's fortress. The Tinman risked all due to his love of his friends. The Lion risked life and limb to try to get Dorothy back to Kansas.

The Wizard did not have the ability to give them a brain, a heart, or courage, but he gave them a task that demonstrated these were already in their possession. He did give them tokens as symbols of these unseen qualities—a diploma, a watch in the shape of a heart, and a medal.

You have been on a journey, too. You have not yet incurred the degree of success that you want in building a life worth living, but if you look over your life in an objective manner, you will see times you have acted in Wise Mind. You did what was rationally intelligent, and at the same time what your gut told you was the right thing to do.

Marsha Linehan points out we all have Wise Mind. DBT skills training helps us to realize when we are in and out of Wise Mind, and how to get back to it when we need to, and how to spend more time in Wise Mind. Don't let any self-critical voices tell you that you don't have Wise Mind. Marsha (like the Wizard) points out that you do.

WISE MIND—WHY WE NEED BOTH REASONABLE MIND AND EMOTION MIND: DEPTH PERCEPTION

Depth perception: it is what allows a baseball player to gauge the speed of a pitch coming towards home plate and time when to swing. It is what allows a driver to realize how far ahead the next car is, and when to hit the brakes.

We have depth perception because we have two eyes, each looking at an object from slightly different perspectives. These slightly contradicting images are then integrated by our brain into a single perception. Without the two different points of view, we would have no depth perception.

Reasonable Mind and Emotion Mind are like two eyes, looking at the world from different perspectives. Only when we put Reasonable Mind and Emotion Mind together to make Wise Mind do we really begin to see our world and ourselves in "3-D."

Star Trek (Roddenberry, 1966) is one of the truly classic science fiction series. The passionate Captain James T. Kirk and the supremely logical science officer Spock often debated back and forth about the best course of action. As such, they illustrate how our Reasonable Mind and Emotion Mind can (and should) have a conversation, a dialogue which brings forth a Wise Minded perspective.

Like your two eyes, Reasonable Mind and Emotion Mind are equally valuable. May your Reasonable and Emotion minds appreciate, value, and, dare I say, love each other the way Kirk and Spock did.

WISE MIND NEEDS EMOTION MIND TO EMPOWER IT

I once went to a workshop by a therapist who told the story of a patient who repeatedly reported engaging in a behavior that was not only immoral and unethical for his profession, but highly illegal. The patient knew with his Reasonable Mind that this behavior was illegal, and knew at an intellectual level that it was in his best interest to stop it, but couldn't bring himself to do this (he loved the behavior). The therapist took him through a guided imagery exercise in which he was arrested by an undercover policeman who catches him in the act. He imagined explaining to his family what he had done, the loss of his professional license, the loss of income, and the loss of dignity and respect by people in the community. As you can imagine, this person felt extreme fear, embarrassment, loss, and shame during this guided imagery session. After this single session, he never engaged in the behavior again, and had a good life.

What happened here? The person's Reasonable Mind understood the potential consequences of the behavior should he be caught: this is why he sought professional help. But without the help of his Emotion Mind, he did not have the strength to make the big change in his behavior. DBT teaches us that emotion serves three purposes, including motivating us to do (or stop doing) things that we otherwise would not have the strength to do. Reasonable Mind needs the strength of Emotion Mind to be wise.

Reasonable Mind needs Emotion Mind's wisdom to be fully Wise-Minded. The above story illustrates how Emotion Mind often has a certain type of wisdom that complements Reasonable Mind. The man's Reasonable Mind knew that he should stop engaging in the behavior, what his Emotion Mind added was the *urgency* and *gravity* of this, that stopping this behavior had to become his number one priority. Our emotions emphasize the urgency of stopping such a self-damaging behavior, and give us the strength to do so.

WISE MIND—HOW DOES EMOTION MIND CONTRIBUTE TO WISE MIND?

Many people coming to DBT are surprised to think that their Emotion Mind is necessary to be in Wise Mind. Their experience is that Emotion Mind is what gets them in trouble, with anger leading to physical fights or insulting remarks, sadness leading to self-harm, etc. Their sense is "emotions = trouble."

It is not Emotion Mind, per se, that gets us into trouble, rather it is Emotion Mind that is not working with Reasonable Mind as a team that leads to self-destructive behavior and negative outcomes.

There is a condition in which people can have a normal level of Reasonable Mind intelligence, or even be very bright, but lack access to Emotion Mind. We call this disorder Autism. Think of the character "Raymond," played by Dustin Hoffman in the Academy Award winning movie, *Rain Man* (Johnson & Levinson, 1988). He is gifted in mathematics, but lacks emotional and social intelligence.

The book *Emotional Intelligence* by Dan Goleman (2006) discusses the importance of emotion in understanding others, and for being effective and successful in our life endeavors. What Coleman refers to as emotional intelligence is a combination of Emotion Mind and Reasonable Mind; in DBT terms, emotional intelligence = Wise Mind.

A final, humorous example of someone being stuck in Reasonable Mind was told to me over thirty years ago by a fellow graduate student. He was working at a church camp, and a famous and distinguished seminary professor was giving the sermon at the evening chapel service. The professor began talking to the middle school campers about "Kierkegaard's teleological suspension of the existential dilemma." The professor was a very intelligent man, but at this moment, not very wise.

REASONABLE MIND NEEDS EMOTION MIND'S WISDOM

I recall listening to one of the immanent researchers on marital satisfaction and marriage therapy tell of a man who had a brain tumor, which had to be removed by surgery. After than man recovered, he was still able to perform complex cognitive tasks, such as balancing his checkbook. However, due to the specific site of the part of his brain that was removed, the man no longer had access to some of his emotional functioning. If given a list of ten tasks to perform during the day, the man was entirely perplexed. He knew how to perform all ten tasks, but he was at a loss as to which to do first. Without his emotions, he could not choose between folding his laundry versus calling 911 because the house was on fire (a very sad story).

This illustrates how we have to simultaneously utilize both Reasonable Mind and Emotion Mind to be in Wise Mind. In a disagreement with my wife, my Reasonable Mind may be able to make persuasive logic-based arguments showing that I am right and she is wrong. However, my Emotion Mind knows if I win the battle of logic but hurt her feelings, at minimum I have gravely damaged, if not destroyed the relationship. My Emotion Mind knows the hurt both she and I will reap if my behavior is informed only by Reasonable Mind. Both Reasonable and Emotion Mind need each other to become Wise Mind.

MINDFULNESS SKILLS—METAPHOR—"YOUR SIX NEW BEST FRIENDS"

In the Mindfulness module, we learn about the three "What" Skills (Linehan, 2015a, p. 53), and the three "How" Skills (Linehan, 2015a, p. 60). When I began teaching DBT skills groups, I did not appreciate these six skills the way I do now. Through the years, I have come to appreciate both their significance and how they, by themselves, have been life transforming for both the persons I taught and myself.

Now when I begin teaching the Mindfulness module, I tell the group, "I am going to introduce you to your new six best friends!" explaining how the Observe, Describe, Participate, Non-Judgmentally, One-Mindfully, and Effectively skills can change the course of their lives in the direction of a life worth living.

Often, I give everyone in the group a dry erase marker (they choose the color) and challenge them to write the six skills (Observe, Describe, Participate, Non-Judgmentally, One-Mindfully, and Effectively on their bathroom mirror. Doing this helps people think about and remember the skills, beginning in the morning, and recall them just before retiring for bed.

OBSERVE AND DESCRIBE—KNOWN FACTS VERSUS JUMPING TO CONCLUSIONS

One of my patients was preparing for her freshman year of college in a faraway state. As part of getting ready for the big transition, she emailed the person who would be her dormitory roommate, someone she had never met, who had been randomly assigned to her by the college. My patient was anxious to get to know what she was like because they would be sharing living quarters for the next year.

The future roommate did not reply. My patient began to worry about what this girl was like. Was she too conceited to reply? Was she a very aloof person to the point that she was ignoring my patient? Was she weird or odd? Would she make the freshman year an extremely awkward and uncomfortable experience? My client was extremely worried, but I encouraged her not to jump to conclusions about this lack of reply. What would you think if you were in my patient's shoes? I encouraged her just to stick with the facts. All that we knew was this girl was assigned to be her roommate, she had an email address, and she did not reply to my client's email. Was she conceded? Aloof? Odd? A number of weeks passed, my patient sent several more emails, but still no reply. My patient's worry grew.

Just before my client left for college, a return email came from the new roommate. She had been on a six-week wilderness canoeing trip with no access to the outside world. Jumping to conclusions creates unneeded worry and sometimes friction. Separating the facts from our interpretations is an extremely valuable skill.

OBSERVE SKILL—MY YOGA EXPERIENCE

When I was in graduate school I took a non-credit course in yoga. One of the first exercises the instructor had us do was to put our thumb about a half inch in front of our eyes, and focus on it, then slowly over a two-minute period pull our thumb away from our head until our arm was fully extended. After this two-minute practice, guess what we did next? We spent two minutes slowly bringing our thumb back to our face, while focusing on it intently. I thought, "This is the stupidest thing I have ever seen! What a waste of time!"

I drove home irked by the yoga class. Once in my apartment, I opened my front window, and was astounded by what I saw…a large tree in full bloom with beautiful white blossoms. It had just rained, and the tree glistened with raindrops as the sun reflected on it. I was so enraptured by the beauty of the tree that I pulled up a chair and sat and looked at it for about 20 minutes, enjoying the beauty. It was one of the happiest experiences of my life.

Then it dawned on me. I had been living directly across the street from this tree for about four years, yet I had never really seen the tree!

This is what mindfulness practice helps us to do: Observe. Many of us (myself included) struggle with a mind that is constantly thinking, chattering away about all sorts to things, creating numerous theories, and our focus is enslaved by this nonstop mind chatter. As a result, we miss out on experiencing our environment. Mindfully observing can bring much joy back into our lives.

OBSERVE SKILL

Most of us do not appreciate the difference between observing someone's behavior versus observing the behavior *then* making a judgment or interpretation. Observing in relationships is just observing behavior, without interpreting the motivation of the person engaging in the behavior.

I once was working with a couple in marital therapy and I observed a consistent pattern that always led to conflict and hurt feelings. The wife would share some issue that greatly troubled her, often something that had nothing to do with the husband. The husband would respond by making a light-hearted joke and chuckling. The wife interpreted this as her husband not taking her problems seriously, making fun of her, even mocking the seriousness of what she had shared. I explored what was going on in the husband when he did this. When the wife would share some painful event, something that he could do nothing about in that moment to help her, he became extremely anxious and often angry (at the source of her troubles). His way of regulating his anxiety and anger was to use humor, making a joke to alleviate his own distress—something most of us do to some degree. His intent was not to trivialize, invalidate, or disrespect his wife. But she assumed it was.

What I did with this couple was help the husband become more mindful of his anxiety, and to do the opposite of his "action urge" of using humor to regulate his emotions. I instructed him to respond with seriousness and compassion. For the wife, it was important not to misperceive that his laughter was motivated by a lack of concern or respect, but that it was actually came out because the great degree to which his wife's distress troubled him. At the same time, I worked with her, using Interpersonal Effective skills (Linehan, 2015a, pp. 117–164) to tell the husband "joking about this hurts me, it is not what I need. What I need is seriousness and compassion."

It is important to observe the behavior of others. But don't make the assumption that you know what their motives are. Ask them their intent.

The animated film *Inside Out* (Docter, 2015), is about a young girl named Riley and her imaginary friend, a clown named Bing Bong. Riley and Bing Bong are riding a train, and on the train is a car that has boxes labeled "Facts" and other boxes labeled "Opinions." The train derails and crashes, and the contents of these boxes spill out. "Oh no!" says Bing Bong, explaining that when facts and opinions get mixed up, they are very hard to correctly sort out. This is a big part of our task with the Observe skill, to just observe without adding interpretations, judgments, and opinions.

OBSERVING JUDGMENTAL THOUGHTS

Today, after a break, I observed my own self talk: "Gotta go back to writing that **stupid** book!" Hopefully by now you are beginning to recognize words like "stupid" as red flags that our mind has slipped into judgmental thinking. I find it very interesting how judgmental thoughts prevent us from accurately **observing** and **describing** our experience. Not only does the judgmental nature of my self-talk make this non-mindful, but it actually obscures what is really going on. A more accurate and mindful self-statement, leading to more self-awareness would be "I choose to go back to writing the DBT book, and I am aware that I have significant feelings of frustration in doing this. This type of writing can be difficult and taxing, leading to frustration." This type of accurate self-observation allows me to understand the issue is my frustration, not the worthiness of the book. Recognizing this allows me to not give up on writing the book, and to cope with the real issue (mental fatigue).

Judgmental self-talk distorts and obscures our view of reality. The accurate perception is not that the book is stupid (at least I hope it's not-Lol), but that I am having an emotional experience called frustration. In my judgmental moment, the locus of **where** the experience was perceived shifted from something inside of me (my emotions) to outside of me (the quality of the book). Do you see what a gross distortion of reality that is? Since beginning mindfulness practice through DBT, I have begun noticing many people **project what is on the inside of themselves** to something or someone on the outside of themselves, and thus greatly misperceive themselves and their world (I include myself in this group). Practicing the Observe and Describe skills in Nonjudgmental fashion cleans this process up, allowing us to see the world as it really is.

OBSERVE AND DESCRIBE NONJUDGMENTALLY—
HOW OUR INTERPRETATION CAN BE INACCURATE

As a psychologist, I often tell my patients that their feelings and/or emotions are seldom wrong, but their perception of events that prompted the emotion can be very wrong. Here is an example of my misperception of a situation.

A friend of mine, Dr Brett Dowdy recruited me to work at the state psychiatric hospital in Cincinnati. Part of adjusting to the new work site was learning their e-mail system. In the first several months I worked there, Brett and I would e-mail each other on tasks and duties of the hospital. As I do in spoken word, I would often put a little humorous twist onto the things I would email to Brett. One day he responded to one of my humor-laced messages by saying "Your e-mails are really weird." I was hurt and outraged! Who was Brett to judge me, telling me how weird I am? When I got home, I told my wife just how livid I was.

The next day I approached Brett and said, "I got your e-mail saying my e-mails were weird." "Yes," said Brett, "every time you send me an e-mail, it pops up as an appointment." I realized I had been clicking the wrong icon when creating an e-mail. I had entirely misinterpreted what Brett was saying to me. My rage instantly disappeared (and I felt a little embarrassed, but not very much because I did not act on my rage).

In DBT you will discover how you have sometimes misperceived events in your life by making judgments (assumptions, jumping to conclusions, categorizing things). All of us fall into the trap of believing these judgments to be facts, when in actuality, they are just our perception in the moment. Sometimes our judgments may be accurate, and yet sometimes they are not. At best, a judgment is a hypothesis to be tested. In DBT you are encouraged to "check the facts" and separate facts from your interpretation of them.

PARTICIPATE SKILL—STAY IN THE PRESENT

The Participate skill includes making sure we are focusing our attention only on the here and now, this very moment.

Ronald D. Siegel, in his book *The Mindfulness Solution* (2010), has a quote from Mark Twain which says, "I am a very old man and have suffered a great many misfortunes, ... most of which never happened."

Many of us torture ourselves by ruminating on what **could** happen, but if we kept a tally of how often these fears actually materialize, we discover virtually none of them do. However, the torment we create for ourselves is very real and tangible. Practicing the Participate skill liberates us from much of our anxiety and worry.

Staying focused in the present is a skill that we develop by practicing. The first step is to realize when our minds have drifted out of the present, something Gestalt therapists call "futurizing." Jesus asked his followers, "Can any of you by worrying add a single hour to your span of life?" (Matthew 6:27, New Revised Standard Version). Jesus explicitly told his followers, "Do not worry about tomorrow for tomorrow will bring worries of its own, today's trouble is enough for today." Jesus was telling his followers to focus on today, solving problems the only place we can, in the present.

Jesus's rhetorical question, "Can any of you, by worrying, add a single hour to your span of life?" is ironic, because not only can we not add an hour to our life, but as psychophysiological research has recently pointed out, worry can shorten our lifespan (Sapolsky, 2010). If you want a longer future, stay in the present!

PARTICIPATE SKILL—MY EXPERIENCE WITH MY TWO SONS

The Participate skill encourages us to be fully present and aware of our current experience right now, in the moment. One of my favorite Marsha Linehan sayings is when she tells us, "When you walk, walk" (Linehan 2015a; Dimeff, 2005). In other words, be fully aware of your legs moving, your feet coming to rest on the ground (including what the surface feels like as your weight shifts to it), and the way your other foot is now pulling back from contact with this surface as it begins to move to replant itself in the next step.

A number of years ago, I had the following experience that illustrates the importance and usefulness of the Participate skill. It was a beautiful autumn day (my favorite time of year). I was sitting on the front porch of our new house, which for me was the dream house I had wished for and worked towards for 30 years. The weather was absolutely perfect; there was warm sunlight that felt good to the skin, yet the gentlest of breezes that kept me comfortable. My two sons, ages two and four, were sitting on either of my legs, hugging me and talking, telling me about a number of things, including how much they loved me.

But then I realized, ... this was not where my mind was. My mind was making lists of things I would need to do the following day, most of it very mundane, such as pick up some paperclips from our Administrative Assistant at work, fill out thus-and-such form, attend a perfunctory meeting, etc. My body was in one of the most wonderful moments of my life, but my mind was somewhere else, ruminating about routine tasks I needed to do the following day. My mind wandered out of utopia.

Human minds wander. This is not bad, it's just what they do. Mindfulness practice includes bringing our awareness back to participate with the here-and-now. When we are not experiencing happiness, joy, and pleasure, the problem often is not so much a lack of good things to enjoy, but rather we are not actively engaged with and focused on the here-and-now of those possibilities.

PARTICIPATE SKILL—HARRY TRUMAN

Immersing ourselves totally in one behavior, fully in the present, ignoring past and future, are the hallmarks of the Participate skill. Author David McCullough (McCullough, 1992) gives us a picture of this in his biography of the 33rd president of the United States, Harry S. Truman.

Truman was elected vice president in 1944; when President Franklin Roosevelt died in 1945, he became the 33rd President of the United States. Three years later, in the spring of 1948, his public approval rating was only 36 percent, and his opponent in the election, governor Thomas Dewey, was way ahead in the polls. To make matters worse, Truman's own political party fractured into three elements, one branch being more liberal, the other more conservative, draining support away from Truman in the middle of the party.

Amidst these bleak realities, President Truman responded by engaging in the Participate skill.

Rather than focus on the polls, he immersed himself totally into discussing the issues that plagued everyday Americans, such as the housing shortage, wages of workers, and inequities in Civil Rights. He embarked on a tour of the entire United States by train, a "whistle-stop" tour, stopping at towns large and small. President Truman would speak to the crowds from the platform on the back of the train. Often he would lay his notes aside and talk directly with scores of people about the issues facing the United States in 1948.

Virtually no one, even inside the Truman campaign, thought he had a chance to win the election. The three major polling organizations (Roper, Crossely, and Gallup) quit polling as early as September and thus failed to detect Truman's growing momentum. The Chicago Tribune newspaper began printing the paper early on election day evening, announcing that Thomas Dewey had won the election.

On Election Day, November 2nd, Truman voted with his wife, had dinner, and went to bed early rather than stay up and watch election returns. The campaigning was over, he had voted and there was nothing more that he could do, so rather than brood and obsess about what was going to happen over the next several hours, he went to sleep. He woke around midnight, turned on the radio, and heard that he was ahead in the popular vote count by one million votes, but newscasters where still predicting that Dewey would win. So, Truman went back to sleep.

By about 4:00 am, newscasters were announcing the stunning upset. Truman had won the popular vote by about two million votes, and won the Electoral College 303 to 189.

The point of the story is not to endorse a political party or candidate. Regardless what you think of Truman's presidency, he gave us an example of the Participate skill. He threw himself fully into talking directly to the American public. He didn't dwell on the recent past such as polls or the editorials of newspaper men. He did not ruminate on what could go wrong on Election Day. He focused on the present, the here and now, immersing himself in the relationship he had with individual voters, speaking from his head and his heart.

The rest, as they say, is history.

PARTICIPATE SKILL—THE SOCK DRAWER

The Participate skill directs us to immerse ourselves totally in what we're doing in the moment, totally in the present. Anxiety and depression happen when we spend a lot of our time obsessing over what *might* happen in the future, or brooding over what happened in the past.

Although I don't know that Marsha Linehan would agree exactly with my numerical estimate, what I tell my DBT group members is it we should spend two to three percent of our time thinking about the future, two to three percent thinking about the past, and 95 percent of our attention should be focused in the present, in the here and now. We do need to think about the future enough to choose our goals, strategies, and actions to get there. We need to spend a little bit of time reflecting on our past, looking at how it shapes our values, valuing the positive relationships and experiences we have had, and reminding ourselves of the mistakes that we don't want to repeat. But 95 percent of the time we should be totally focused in the present.

I like comparing focusing on the past and future to having a sock drawer. When used correctly, sock drawers are very useful. The key is to put clean socks into the drawer, then get out and shut the drawer. Return to it only when you need a clean pair of socks. Likewise, when you to reflect on the past or think about future goals, do so, but then get out and live in the present. Don't spend the bulk of your day fooling around in the sock drawer.

PARTICIPATE IN THE PRESENT—JEDI WISDOM

The wise Jedi Master, Yoda, in *Star Wars: Episode V – Empire Strikes Back* (Lucas & Kershner, 1980), said of Luke Skywalker that all his life he has looked away, to the future, to the horizon saying he never focused his mind on where he was and what he was doing.

This statement from Yoda happens as he guides Luke Skywalker on his quest to find Yoda. Luke doesn't realize that this small creature with a wacky sense of humor is actually the person he is looking for. Brooding about the past or the future takes our head out of the only game where we can directly observe and directly influence: the present. To borrow a phrase from the 1960s, the present "is where it's at!"

Acceptance and Commitment Therapy (Hayes, Strosahl, & Wilson, 2012) points out that humans' ability to think about and conceptualize the future is both a tremendous advantage and also potentially a tremendous pitfall. It is a tremendous advantage because it helps us plan for the future and engage in problem solving. It can be a potential tremendous pitfall because we can worry about all sorts of things that never happen. If you are a habitual worrier, it can be an interesting exercise to begin cataloging all the catastrophes you have imagined, and then see how many actually ever happen. Occasionally the answer is one, but more often it is zero.

When he made his statement, Yoda was pointing out how Luke's mind continually wandered into the future, and if he were to become a Jedi, he would need to change this mental behavior by bringing his awareness into the present.

This Jedi wisdom serve you well it will, young Padawan.

EFFECTIVELY SKILL—EVEN ROCK STARS NEED THIS

To practice the Effectively skill, we must start by identifying what we want to accomplish. Only when we have clearly defined our goal do we have a context for determining what behaviors will be effective for achieving that goal, and conversely, what behaviors will be counterproductive.

Sometimes we can have multiple goals, and we may need to prioritize one goal over other goals. This is a story of a person who had to do just that.

John Mellencamp was a young man in his early twenties when he decided that he wanted to pursue music as a full-time career rather than as a hobby. He made a demo tape and headed to New York to talk to agents and record companies. At first, no one was interested, but he went back several times, and finally one solitary agent thought he possessed some potential and offered him a contract. Mellencamp signed the contract without carefully reading all the details. The agent got him a record deal, he recorded an album, and a huge kickoff for his career was set up for his hometown of Seymour, Indiana. It was while preparing for the release of his first album that Mellencamp discovered a huge problem: his agent/manager had decided that it would be impossible to market someone in the music industry with the name John Mellencamp, and so he changed his stage name to "Johnny Cougar" (Johnson, 2007, p. 20).

Mellencamp was angry that his name had been changed to "Johnny Cougar" with this name affixed to his album. He hated the name. Here is where he had to decide which goal was more important: getting his music out to others and becoming a star, or shed the dreaded "Johnny Cougar" label. Mellencamp decided that having a shot at a career in rock music was his most important goal, so he radically accepted that he would be called "Johnny Cougar" for the foreseeable future.

Johnny Cougar's first album was a flop. It received poor reviews, and sold few copies. Mellencamp himself acknowledged he did not know anything at this juncture about making an album, let alone a good one. The album did so poorly that the record company dropped him. His agent was able to negotiate a second deal with another record company. At this juncture, Mellencamp was able to negotiate (a skill we will discuss in the Interpersonal Effectiveness module as a "DEAR MAN" skill) a small change in his name. He would be henceforth be billed simply as "John Cougar." He was willing to take what he could get.

At the second record company "John Cougar" had several modest hits (three songs in the Billboard Top 40). The albums during this period did moderately well, but not enough for him to have the leverage to reclaim his real name. In 1982, he had another album to give to the record company, titled *American*

Fool. The record company did not like the album, and wanted him to re-record it, but Mellencamp stood his ground, insisting it be released in its original form. American Fool was the biggest selling album in 1982 (five million copies), contained three big hit singles, and won a Grammy. After eight long years in the recording industry, Mellencamp had enough leverage to have his name be listed as "John Cougar Mellencamp" on his next album. He negotiated and got some of what he wanted, but he was not able to jettison the dreaded "Cougar". After seven more years and tens of millions of albums sold worldwide, he was able to release an album as simply "John Mellencamp."

Mellencamp's journey illustrates the Effectively skill. We must decide what our most important goal is, and choose our behavior in the light of what will be effective to achieve that goal. We will need to refrain from behaviors that would compromise our goal. Asking our self, "Will this help me reach my goal, or will it undermine my goal?" is the key to practicing the Effectively skill. You will not win every battle, but this skill will help you win the war.

EFFECTIVELY SKILL—LETTING GO OF VENGEFUL DESIRES

In a previous unpublished version of the Second Edition of the DBT workbook that I was made privy to, there was a bullet point under the Effectively skill that did not make the final edit. It read, "Let go of vengeance, useless anger and [self] righteousness that hurts you and doesn't work." Vengeful emotions and behaviors bog us down, and are the antithesis of being effective.

In Super Bowl XLV, I watched the early part of the game in which the Green Bay Packers quarterback Aaron Rodgers threw several excellent passes only to have them dropped by his receivers. Green Bay had to punt, and I thought that if I were Aaron Rodgers, I would be enraged. I watched with amazement as Rogers shook off these disappointments and continued to be supportive of his receivers. As the game wore on, they began catching his passes with greater accuracy and Green Bay won the Super Bowl. It seems to me that Aaron Rodgers chose to be effective rather than hold grudges or stew in self-righteousness.

Umpires and referees are not perfect. They will make mistakes and an athlete can begin to ruminate about the unfairness of a particular call. Effective athletes know that when they cannot change the call, it is most effective to let this injustice pass, and focus on the next play. If you are dwelling on vengeful fantasies, this will undermine your effectiveness, which is why we choose to let go of vengefulness.

EFFECTIVELY SKILL—MAKING A BUBBLE HAT

When my son Noah was about three years old, he was demonstrating that very predictable behavior of asserting himself and saying "no" to much of what I told him to do. All children do this, and it is actually part of normal psychological development.

I was giving Noah a bath, and it was going pretty well until I told him we needed to wash his hair. As can be expected, Noah strongly said "no!" He did this in large part due to his fear of getting soap in his eyes. I could have got into a power struggle with him, exerted my superior physical strength and forced him to wash his hair. But I decided not to. I chose to not get in a struggle of "I am right and you are wrong."

What I did was to tell him, "You do not have to wash your hair," but then several minutes later asked if he had ever had a bubble hat. His eyes lit up, "What's a bubble hat?" "Here let me show you," I said, and I took bubbles from the bubble bath and piled them on my head. Now Noah was pleading with me for his own bubble hat, and soon the bubbles were piled very high on his head.

I let him look in the mirror at his hat. He was extremely proud of what a fanciful hat we had constructed. Then we rinsed it off and got out of the bathtub.

What was my objective in this situation? In the short term I wanted Noah to have clean hair. Secondly, I wanted him to overcome (rather than be mastered by) his fear of getting soap in his eyes. Lastly, I wanted to help him realize that in the big picture, "father knows best," and that he could trust my advice in spite of his fears.

I had already begun to teach DBT skills, and was beginning to appreciate the wisdom of being effective in getting my objective accomplished over being "right." This is a huge paradigm shift that can make your life a lot simpler, easier, and more successful.

EFFECTIVELY SKILL—A PARADIGM SHIFT

Choosing to do what is effective can be a tremendous paradigm shift. Over the last several decades, there has been tremendous public debate over needle exchange programs for IV drug users. Many people see such a program as "wrong," and programs that are publicly funded are seen as using taxpayer money in "aiding and abetting" people in illicit drug use. What you think about this issue may be, in large degree, determined by your paradigm or the way in which you view the world.

In DBT, we choose to ask the question "What is *effective*?" In the case of needle exchange programs, one would ask, what is our goal? If the goal is to reduce the incidence of HIV and hepatitis C, then needle exchange programs do make sense because the scientific research does show that they reduce the transmission of these diseases (Greenwood, 2018; Harper, 2015), including, in some cases, to the unborn children if the addict is a pregnant woman. This is where my personal morality is informed by the Effectively skill. I do not want anyone, innocent or not, to be infected with HIV or hepatitis C. Some of the people who receive the exchanged needles will go on to successfully recover from their addiction. There is no scientific evidence that withholding clean needles from drug users somehow makes addicts more likely to kick the habit—in fact, the preliminary research suggests the opposite. There is no scientific evidence that suggests that giving people clean needles encourages them to continue their drug addiction or make them less likely to sooner or later pursue abstinence. My personal viewpoint, informed by the DBT

Effectively skill (Linehan, 2015a, p. 60), is to **do what works** for the benefit of humanity.

Another example of this concerns the Dalai Lama. My understanding is that, for most of his life, the Dalai Lama chose to be a vegetarian out of his devotion to compassion for all living creatures. However, when he developed a health condition, his physician advised him that there would be a nutritional advantage to eat an occasional serving of meat, and so he changed his practice. He chose to do what worked.

Much of my clinical practice involves family therapy and couples' therapy. Much of the conflict and agony in these relationships stems from all parties involved being focused on proving themselves right and the other person wrong. Once I can bring this power struggle over proving who is right and wrong to an end, the relationships heals. There are other skills that need to be learned for satisfying relationships, but none of them work if people are primarily invested in being "right."

When we are invested in "being right" or proving other people wrong, we have strayed from the Effectively path, and reap a harvest of suffering. All of us have had periods of where we were more interested in "winning" an argument, proving the other person "wrong" and being "right" rather than doing what is effective.

I have traveled both paths. But my life got much easier and happier when I switched to the Effectively path.

EFFECTIVELY SKILL: POUNDING THE TV

When I grew up in the 1960s, there were no flat screen TVs. Televisions were huge, bulky contraptions, and they were not as reliable as they are today. TV's malfunctioned more often, with the picture skipping up and down or becoming very fuzzy.

When a TV began malfunctioning in the middle of a TV show, many people, filled with frustration, would get up and smack the TV with their hand. Occasionally this would jar the TV back into synch, but 99 out of 100 times all it did was just make the TV more unstable as it jarred loose the fragile tubes and welded circuitry that comprised the inner workings of these Neanderthal entertainment boxes.

Hitting the TV did not make it work better, but it may have made the owner feel a little better for a few brief seconds.

Much of our behavior may be like punching an ancient TV. It may feel like the right thing to do, but doing so may be taking us farther away from our goal.

This is where the Mindfulness Effectively skill (Linehan, 2015a, p. 60) is extremely useful. First, ask yourself what it is you're trying to accomplish. Then assess whether your behavior is actually effective in getting you to that goal. If it is not, simply lay it aside and choose a behavior that is effective in moving you towards your goal.

Once this skill becomes second nature, you will find yourself sorting all of your behavior through the prism of the Effectively skill. Behaviors and attitudes are either effective for what we want to accomplish or they are ineffective. If your life has been a frustrating experience, it may be because many of your behaviors are in the non-effective category.

LOVING KINDNESS PRACTICE—DID YOU EXPECT IT HERE?

Mindfulness Handout 8 (Linehan, 2015a, p. 70) is "Practicing Loving Kindness to Increase Love and Compassion." This handout points out "loving kindness can protect us from developing and holding on to judgmentalness, ill-will, and hostile feelings towards **ourselves** and **others**" (Linehan, 2015a, p. 70; emphasis mine).

Linehan instructs us to start with either someone else we want to love or with ourselves, and achieve some mastery in developing loving kindness to ourselves or to those who we love. Only after we have acquired some skill in directing loving kindness to people we love, do we move on to try to extend it to those who frustrate, hurt, or anger us. Sending a message of loving kindness to those difficult persons requires more skill and practice in Loving Kindness.

Some people are reticent to embrace the practice of loving kindness because it appears to them to be ultra-idealistic, impractical, and not possible in the real world. Others rightly discern that this DBT practice stems from Buddhism and other eastern philosophies.

For some persons, the eastern philosophical roots coupled with the lofty goal of having compassion for everyone is a deal-breaker. Some, whose commitment is to Western religious ideals such as Christianity, feel that indiscriminately adopting such ideas from Eastern religions is antithetical to their religion. If this description fits your reaction to Loving Kindness practice, consider the words of Jesus in Matthew's gospel (chapter 5 beginning with verse 44). Jesus said, "**Love your enemies, bless them that curse you, do good to them who hate you, pray for them who despitefully use you and persecute you.**"

This sounds like *advanced* loving kindness practice to me.

REFERENCES

Brooks, J L, Groening, M, & Simon, S (Executive Producers). (1989) *The Simpsons*. [Television Series]. Gracie Films, 20th Century Fox Television, & Twentieth Century Fox.

Brown, D (Producer), & Beresford, B (Director). (1989) *Driving Miss Daisy* [Motion Picture]. United States: The Zanuck Company, Allied Filmmakers, & Majestic Films International.

Docter, P (Director). (2015) *Inside Out*. Walt Disney Pictures. Dimeff, L. (Producer). (2005). From chaos to freedom [Motion picture]. United States: Dawkins Production.

Dimeff, L (Producer). (2005) *From chaos to freedom*. United States: Dawkins Production.

Fleming, V (Director). (1939) *The Wizard of Oz*. Metro-Goldwyn-Meyer.

Goleman, D. (2006) *Emotional intelligence: Why it can matter more than IQ*. New York, NY, US: Bantam Dell.

Greenwood, M. (2018) *New study finds HIV outbreak in Indiana could have been prevented*. Retrieved from news.yale.edu/2018/09/13/new-study-finds-hiv-outbreak-indiana-could-have-been-prevented

Harper, J. (2015) *Indiana's HIV outbreak leads to reversal on needle exchanges*. Retrieved from /www.npr.org/sections/health-shots/2015/06/02/411231157/indianas-hiv-outbreak-leads-to-reversal-on-needle-exchanges

Hayes, S C, Strosahl, K D, & Wilson, K G. (2012) *Acceptance and commitment therapy: The process and practice of mindful change* (2nd ed.). New York, NY, US: Guilford Press.

Johnson, H. (2007) *John Mellencamp: The story*. Omnibus Press, New York.

Johnson, M (director) & Levinson, B. (1988) *Rain Man*. United Artists.

Kirkwood, G (Producer), & Avildsen, J G (Director). (1976) *Rocky* [Motion Picture]. United States: Chartoff-Winkler Productions.

Linehan, M M. (1993) *Skills training manual for treating borderline personality disorder*. New York: Guilford.

Linehan, M M. (2015a) *DBT skills training handouts and worksheets*. New York, Guilford.

Linehan, M M. (2015b) *DBT skills training manual*. New York: Guilford.

Lucas, G (Producer) & Kershner, I (Director). (1980) *Star Wars: Episode v – the empire strikes back* [Motion Picture]. United States: Lucasfilm.

Lynch, T R. (2018) *Radically open dialectical behavioral therapy: Theory and practice for treating disorders of overcontrol*. Oakland, CA, US: Context Press/New Harbinger Publications.

McCullough, D. (1992) *Truman*. Simon and Shuster. New york

Morris, M J, Johns, L C, & Oliver, J E. (2013) *Acceptance and commitment therapy and mindfulness for psychosis*. West Sussex: John Wiley and Sons.

Roddenberry, G (Executive Producer & Creator). (1996) *Star Trek* [Television Series]. United States: Desilu Productions, Norway Corporation, & Paramount Television.

Sapolsky, R. (2010) *The great courses: Stress and your body*. The Teaching Company. Chantilly, VA

Siegel, R D. (2010) *The mindfulness solution: Everyday practices for everyday problems*. New York, NY, US: Guilford Press.

Interpersonal Effectiveness

Chapter 3

MYTHS THAT INTERFERE WITH INTERPERSONAL EFFECTIVENESS—METAPHOR OF THE TERMITES

Before delving in to the three goals of Interpersonal Effectiveness (Objective Effectiveness, Relationship Effectiveness, Self-Respect Effectiveness) Marsha Linehan directs us to look for myths that interfere with Interpersonal Effectiveness (Linehan, 2015, p. 119).

When I introduce the myths, I draw a picture of a termite on the board. (I am not a very good artist, and the group usually can discern that it is an insect, but not a termite). Once the group is enlightened that this is, in fact, a termite, we discuss the meaning of this metaphor. It matters not how good one's carpentry is, nor the high quality of the wood. If termites invade, they will destroy the structure.

Myths that interfere with Interpersonal Effectiveness are like termites. If you hold beliefs like "I don't deserve to get what I want or need," "asking for what I want is pushy and not nice," or "I shouldn't have to ask for what I want, they should just know it," all the skills training in the world will not help you. Look for the presence of any of these termites, and exterminate them so that you have a safe environment to construct your relationships.

Read through the list of myths that interfere with Interpersonal Effectiveness. Don't let the termites destroy your relationship house.

MYTHS THAT INTERFERE WITH INTERPERSONAL EFFECTIVENESS #9 AND #10 VERSUS "MARCH OF THE PENGUINS"

Myths #9 and #10 (Linehan 2015, p. 119) have something in common. They read as follows: "I must be really inadequate if I can't fix this myself" and "If I would just learn how to think differently, I wouldn't have to bother everybody else." Simply stated, these myths say we should be completely independent and self-sufficient, not needing the help of others.

Some of us have been raised to be ultra-independent, to rely as little as possible on others to get our emotional needs met. Others of us have adopted this myth as a way to protect ourselves from being disappointed or betrayed. In reality, we do need close relationships to be psychologically healthy.

The 2005 film *March of the Penguins* (Jacquet, 2005) documents the yearly reproductive cycle of emperor penguins (it won the Academy Award for Best Documentary). The penguins mate at the same breeding ground each year, and as winter approaches, the females/mothers leave the males with the eggs to return to the sea (100 kilometers/62 miles) to fish for the family. The fathers' job is to tend to their egg, keeping it warm in the dead of the winter when temperatures drop to as low as -60•C or -80•F.

In the dead of winter, these temperatures can easily kill the adult male penguin as well as the unhatched chicks. How do they survive? The colony's males, perhaps several hundred, huddle together in a tightly clustered circle to shield each other from the cold wind and conserve body heat for the group as a whole. The penguins on the outside of the circle are exposed to the -80• temperatures, and would die if they spent more than 15 minutes or so on the periphery of the circle. The penguins work cooperatively, with the outside ring of penguins rotating into the center of the circle every 15 minutes to regain warmth, while other penguins take their turn on the outside, absorbing the bitter cold. By working together, the males along with their eggs survive the brutal winter.

Our experience as humans is different, but in some ways the same. We do not struggle against thermal cold in the same way the penguins do, but we are often confronted with a world that can be emotionally cold. Our metaphoric language reflects this—we talk about "the cold hard facts of life" or "he gave her the cold shoulder." Life can be cold and dark, with phases of our life being winter-like. Reflect on your own experience: you have probably felt very cold at times.

Which brings us back to Myth #10. Nobody stays alive by themselves. We all need to create a circle of people in our lives who take turns with us, shielding each other from the cold realities that life presents. Without a big enough circle, you will spend most of your life shivering.

Recognize this myth for what it is—a falsehood—and shift to the truth. **You do need healthy relationships**, and this module will help you become *effective* at acquiring and maintaining the relationships you need.

INTERPERSONAL EFFECTIVENESS—HAS SOMEONE CALLED YOU "MANIPULATIVE?"

One of the most hurtful things one person can say to another is "you are manipulative!" In most cases, I think such statements are over-simplified, lacking specificity and clarity of focus. The truth is, all of us are trying to manipulate people in our social environment all day long. I try to influence others to do what I want and give me what I want.

Trying to influence others was described in a classic book by Dale Carnegie, *How to Win Friends and Influence People* (1998). Winning friends and influencing people is what all of us have been trying to do all our life. The Interpersonal Effectiveness module will help you to become *more effective* in your efforts, including doing so in a way that does not anger or frustrate other people, and that does not compromise your values.

If other people have accused you of being "manipulative," they probably want a different set of behaviors from you, but don't know how to ask. The Interpersonal Effectiveness module will directly teach you skills to ask for what you want and say "no" to what you don't.

One of the skills highlighted in the DEAR MAN skill set (Linehan, 2015, pp. 125–126) is the "A" which is "Assert" what you want (one could simply say "Ask" for what you want). This may seem like a no-brainer, but there is more to this than first meets the eye. Often people are frustrated with us when we demand or insinuate that they "should" do something we want. Some people try to use guilt or shame to influence people into doing what they want. If we use this approach, we are denying an important truth: in many—if not most—situations, the other person does not owe us what we want. Telling them that they "should" do this comes across as arrogant and controlling.

It takes a degree of humility to acknowledge that we are in a position where we are *asking* for their help. If we acknowledge this dynamic in the relationship, people usually do not feel resentful or put upon. If we *ask,* they are a lot more likely to give us what we want and furthermore to enjoy doing so. Even when the other person is bound by a social contract to give us what we want (in my case, a student under my supervision or an employee), it is usually more effective to ask rather than tell them to do this. I choose to do this simply because it is more effective. In other words, when I use this approach, I get what I want more often and more easily.

Another skill comes from the acronym GIVE (Linehan, 2015, p. 128), namely "be Gentle." As will see in the DBT workbook, this includes refraining from verbal or physical attacks, threats, judgments, and facial expressions like sneering and rolling your eyes. If someone perceives you as strong-arming them into doing what you want, their natural response will be to resist you. Some of us are socialized to think of harsh, forceful behavior as strong, decisive, or "manly," but a great deal of social science research points that all this typically is does stirs up is resentment and resistance (Miller & Rollnick, 2013).

Being gentle communicates that you want to interact with the other person in a collaborative, rather than a coercive manner.

The third set of skills, the FAST skills (Linehan, 2015, p. 130) points to being Fair to others, approaching the relationship with a Win/Win viewpoint rather than trying to get the better of someone. The old adage that "your reputation will precede you" is relevant here. When we put something over on someone, we may win the initial battle, but we lose the big war. The "T" in FAST (be Truthful; Linehan, 2015; p. 130) is also extremely important. Most people don't resent us asking for what we want as long as they know that we are not being deceitful in the process.

Lastly, remember it's important to realize that none of us get what we want 100 percent of the time. It is important to Radically Accept this truth, realizing that even when we don't get what we want in a specific situation, our life can still be worth living.

THE THREE GOALS OF THE INTERPERSONAL EFFECTIVENESS MODULE: THE THREE-LEGGED STOOL

I begin the Interpersonal Effectiveness Module by drawing a stool with three legs and asking the group "What happens if one of the legs breaks?" It is easy to understand that a stool, with only two functional legs, is worthless.

Interpersonal Effectiveness is a three-legged stool. The three legs are **Objective Effectiveness** (asking for what you want in a relationship), **Relationship Effectiveness** (not harming or destroying the relationship, and if possible, strengthening it), and **Self-Respect Effectiveness** (not damaging your self-respect to get what you want). If you are good at only two of the three skill sets, your relationship life will be most unsatisfying. Think about these examples.

Objective Effectiveness: If you are not getting what you want in a relationship, why be in it at all? Some people may think that wanting and expecting something from relationships is selfish (note: this is a myth that interferes with Interpersonal Effectiveness), but if you have been taught this, you have been taught a damaging myth.

In every healthy relationship, both parties want and get something. My employer wants 40 hours of work out of me, I want to be paid fairly and provided the opportunity to practice psychology. In my rock-and-roll band, I want the drummer to set a steady beat, the bass player to play the right notes, and the singers to sing on-key and with passion. They expect me and the other guitar player to play the right notes and chords. I expect my DBT co-leader to lead mindfulness exercises and facilitate homework review; she expects me to pay her.

Relationship Effectiveness: it is possible to get what we want in a relationship, yet wind up damaging and even destroying the relationship. What does it matter if I get my DBT co-leader to help me with specific task if I destroy the relationship, and have to start over with another co-leader? What good is it if I get the band I am in to play a song that only I want to play, but after the show they kick me out of the band?

Some people get their way in romantic relationships by bullying their partner, but the quality of the relationship is very unsatisfying. If the passive partner is willing to put up with abrasive, insulting, invalidating behavior of their partner, the relationship may continue, but it is habitat of misery.

Self-Respect Effectiveness: you can get what you want from a relationship, and the relationship can remain secure, but if you are sacrificing your self-respect by compromising your values, you will not be a happy camper. I have worked with women who have remained in relationships in which their partner demanded they engage in sexual acts they found degrading. Likewise, I have known persons who felt compelled to permit their partner to verbally abuse and humiliate them whenever they were angry. Sometimes individuals sacrifice their dignity at work, feeling pressured to go along with practices they see as unethical.

The trick in Interpersonal Effectiveness is to have three sturdy legs on the stool. It is true there will be times when we choose to sacrifice part of a leg for the sake of the other two. I, for example, have tolerated demeaning bosses to continue employment and thus earn a paycheck and support myself, but most of the time we can attain all three if we practice our skills mindfully.

OBJECTIVE EFFECTIVENESS: TWO SIDES TO THIS COIN

When beginning to learn about Objective Effectiveness, it is important to realize we are talking about two sides of a coin. This skill is about both asking for what you want, and saying "no" to what you don't want.

Often we do not get what we want in a relationship because… we simply do not ask for it.

We may drop hints, or hope that if the other person is really in tune with our thoughts and needs, and that somehow they will magically divine the mystery of what we want. Part of the beauty of this set of skills is that it forces us to hone in on what we specifically want, and then express this with precise words. My experience with a number of people is that they may be very dissatisfied with a relationship, but they have not really focused on what they *specifically want* from the relationship. The "A" skill in DEAR MAN (Assert, or as I often say, Ask) forces us to focus on specifically asserting what it is we want, rather than complain in generalities.

The other side of the coin is saying "no" to what we don't want. This side is just as important as the Assert side. Tonight in my DBT group, the three women present began talking about how they are pressured by men for their phone numbers, dates, romantic encounters, and the like. One said that after she says no, usually the man will keep badgering her, playing the part of a wounded puppy, which results in her feeling guilty about saying "no." My immediate reaction to hearing this was to quote the sentiment of a country song: asks what part of 'no' does the other person not understand?

Saying "no" to what you do not want (and standing your ground) is just as important as specifically asking for what you do want.

OBJECTIVE EFFECTIVENESS—SAYING "NO" TO WHAT YOU DON'T WANT IN A RELATIONSHIP

Half of Relationship Effectiveness is asking for what you want. Sometimes we underestimate the other side of the coin: saying "no" to what we don't want is just as important.

I find many people who have been in my DBT skills groups have not been effective in saying "no" to requests by others, in situations ranging from being asked to do something for a worthy cause, to engaging in sexual activities. Many persons have been socialized to believe that saying "no" is a bad thing (e.g., "you *should* always help out when asked!" or "don't say no to me young lady!") "Saying no = bad" is a very un-dialectical point of view—in truth, all of us need to have the right to refuse things when our Wise Mind tells us so.

I once worked with a man who was very nice; he always tried to help others. Unfortunately, he was so locked into feeling obliged to help others, that he would never tell someone "no," even when he needed some rest. This man would join a church, and soon people would ask him to help in some capacity, he would always say "yes" with a smile, even when he felt uncomfortable or overloaded. He believed that saying "no" was bad, but would become very agitated when loaded down with these requests. Because he had such strong feelings against saying no to requests by a church for help, when he became completely overloaded, he would not assert himself, he would just transfer to a new church. I tried to get him to role play with me saying "no," but he felt so guilty about the word, that he refused to even say it. Sadly, he would not even say "no" to the role play, he just kind of bumbled around, not getting to the "no".

In this DBT module, you will role play in groups saying "no" to requests you choose to decline, and doing so in a confident manner. If you feel tense and uncomfortable in the role play, you are doing this well, exposing yourself to what has been a barrier that is anchored by irrational and unreasonable guilty feelings. By exposing yourself to these feelings while practicing a new, effective behavior, you will prevail in adding the "no" skill to your toolbox.

DEAR MAN—DESCRIBE THE SITUATION

The D in DEAR MAN (Linehan, 2015, p. 125) stands for **Describe** *the situation.* When you ask for something in a relationship, it is important to first build a mutual context between you and the person you're talking to. In the Describe skill, you start with what both you and the other person acknowledge as true. You stick with just the facts of the situation. For example, one of my sons could say to me, "Dad, you asked me to work on my grades, and during the school year I've got nothing but A's and B's." Notice everything in this statement is factual, nothing is up for debate. I did ask him to try to improve his grades, his report card has the factual information. There is nothing to be disputed. The D skill gets the process started on common ground. Opinions have been avoided at this stage of the DEAR process.

DEAR MAN—EXPRESS YOUR FEELINGS AND OPINIONS

One of the most influential philosophers and theologians of the twentieth century was Martin Buber, who discussed what he called the "I-Thou" relationship (Richards & Bergin, 2005, p. 106; Miller, 1999, p. 228). My understanding of what Buber was saying is that much of spirituality is understanding *who I am* and communicating that to someone else, while, at the same time, *recognizing who they are*—their own unique identity and personhood. It places importance on both the "I" and the "Thou" being in the presence of each other.

You will notice that under the Express skill (Linehan, 2015, p. 125), Dr Linehan encourages us to use statements like "I want" or "I feel" rather than statements like "people should pick up after themselves." She is coaching us towards having an "I-Thou" relationship as part of Interpersonal Effectiveness, rather than "it-that".

At the end of many wedding ceremonies, the minister will conclude by saying something to the effect of "Now *by the authority granted* to me by the state of Ohio, I now pronounce you husband and wife." When you make a request of someone else you do so *by the authority of your feelings*. It is an "I-Thou" request. It is based on the fact that *you* are in a relationship with this other person and your feelings are telling you what you want, just as the other person's emotions tell them what they want.

If you experience some of your relationships as boring and hollow, it may be that you and the other person have slipped into an "it-that" way of communicating. You are talking about virtually everything *except yourselves*. These types of relationships are limited to living on the periphery, but not at the heart of one's life. People who limit their focus to things, avoiding sharing their emotions (as popular vernacular suggests) never get to the *heart* of the matter.

The name of the module is Interpersonal Effectiveness. When you express your feelings/emotions, you are bringing the *personal* into the inter-personal.

DEAR MAN—EXPRESS SKILL

The E in DEAR MAN is **Express** *your feelings and emotions*. It may seem that you have moved from the facts of the situation in the Describe skill to the realm of the non-factual (emotions), but this is not the case. It is a *fact* that this is *how you feel*. The fact that you feel this way is not up for argument between you and the other person, it is a fact. You are not telling them that they should feel the same way that you do, you are simply letting them know what your own internal GPS is saying to you.

The **Express** skill is very important in asking for what you want, or conversely for what you want to say no to. Say, for example, my wife wants to go to the Opera, but I have no interest in the Opera. If she tells me, "Jim, I would really *love* to go to the Opera this weekend," she is giving me the reason to go, and she really does not need to give me any other reason. When two people are in a relationship of any kind, if they are Wise-Minded, they honor the other person's emotions. My wife should not have to persuade me with logic that going to the

Opera is the "right" thing to do. She loves the Opera, that by itself is powerful enough to persuade me.

If you have been through the Emotion Regulation module, you know that emotion has three purposes: it communicates to ourselves, it communicates to others, and it motivates us. The reason that we invoke our emotion at the Express stage of DEAR MAN is motivational; if another person is to change their behavior at our request, we need to motivate them, which means persuading them on an emotional level. By expressing our emotions, we are communicating the importance of our request. Even though at the E stage of DEAR MAN we have not yet specifically asked for what we want, by expressing the E, we are setting the table for this in the next step, Assert (or Ask). Our emotions and our opinions are the *compelling* part of our request.

DEAR MAN: ASSERT OR ASK

Between two stints of graduate school, I had a job interviewing candidates for sales positions for a major US corporation. I learned many interesting and important things about the world of sales. One was the importance of "ask for the order." A salesperson cannot be shy or beat around the bush when talking about their products. They need to have a good sense of when to ask, "How many of these should we order for you?"

The same is true when we think of the A in DEAR MAN. Much of the time **Assert** means **asking,** but Assert also includes saying "no!"

Often people don't get what they want from others because they simply don't come out and ask for what they want. They wish that others would somehow intuitively know what they want. I once engaged in this kind of wishful thinking. I was working for a very troubled church. The church had a great deal of infighting, had lost members, and there was a significant drop in both attendance and offerings. They could no longer afford a full-time minister, and so they hired me, a graduate student in psychology with a seminary background, and I went to work as their interim minister. In about a year and a half, I turned the congregation completely around, helping it become harmonious, and the attendance and offering went back up. I left to go on my psychology internship and secretly wished that they would express their gratitude by buying me the guitar of my dreams, a Fender Telecaster. They knew I was a guitar player and somehow, I believed, this would be good enough to make this happen. But I never came out and said, "If you really want to express your appreciation, a Fender Telecaster would be an excellent way to do so." I not did ask. My last Sunday came, and alas, no Telecaster. Why? Because I did not use the "A" word, I did not *ask* for what I wanted.

Also remember that telling somebody to do something for you is very different than asking. With the **A (Assert)** skill we are telling the person what we want, and asking them to give it to us. Demanding things, in most cases, makes it less likely that we will get what we want. Also, by asking rather than telling the person to do something, we are acknowledging, with some humility, that we are in the asking position. People do not like to be bossed around or coerced. When we try to push people into what we want, it is more likely that they will push back rather than try to honor the demand. If we ask somebody for something, we are more likely to receive it.

DEAR MAN: REINFORCE—A JUICY CARROT

When I explain the R in DEAR MAN, I start by drawing a picture of a carrot on the dry erase board. The R in DEAR MAN is **Reinforce**, a behavior modification term. A synonym for reinforce is the word **reward.** The Reinforce skill tells us to reward people for giving us what we want (or for accepting "no" for an answer).

One of the hallmarks of any successful interpersonal relationship is that it is a Win/Win scenario. We are thinking not only about ourselves, but about the other person; we want both parties to be winners and gain something important from the interaction (notice how dialectical this is). When we conclude our DEAR with a reward, we are showing the other person what is in it for them.

So, back to the carrot metaphor. When we ask for something, we want to dangle a carrot in front of the other person, showing what's in it for them. They may have already been inclined to give us what we want, but why not increase the probability of success by sweetening the deal?

My DBT group members typically struggle when initially trying to apply this skill, because they are at a loss for what to dangle as the carrot. The truth is, one of the most rewarding things we can give someone else, is an expression of our appreciation. Often, we cannot offer some sort of monetary reward, but what we can say is "I would appreciate if you wash your own dishes rather than leaving them in the sink. If you do that I will continue to enjoy being your roommate."

Last summer my family and some friends drove 250 miles to a Cleveland Indians baseball game. We did not know it, but they were giving away Cleveland Indians souvenir blankets to the first 10,000 in attendance. We got the blankets, but after the game, a couple approached us and explained that they grew up in Cleveland, and had driven all the way from Ft. Worth Texas for the game, but they did not get a blanket. They offered us $30.00 for one of our blankets. Without pausing, my friend Mike gave them one of his family's blankets, but declined the $30.00. The family was thrilled. As we left that day, my friend left with a *reward* that was a lot more than $30.00—the couple's heartfelt appreciation.

People often believe other people are motivated primarily by money, but the scientific research shows that, even in work settings, when a certain minimum financial threshold is met, people are more motivated by social connection, the sense of doing meaningful and important work, and an opportunity to be creative, rather than simply money (Pink, 2009). The same is true for being appreciated by others. Think of your own situation: when someone shares their heartfelt appreciation, what does that do for you? More than money, people like to be liked and appreciated. How is that for a juicy and delicious carrot?

DEAR MAN: STAY MINDFUL SKILL—TRASH TALK

If you have played basketball (or perhaps another sport), you have experienced the phenomenon known as "trash talk." An opponent talks at you constantly, sometimes about random and silly topics, often with insults and challenges. What is the trash-talker trying to do? The answer is one word: *distract* you—he or she is trying to divert your attention from what you are trying to accomplish.

When we use our DEAR MAN skills, people will go sometimes go on tangents, talking about things that take the discussion off of our goal. Sometimes this is intentional (like trash talk) Most of the time it is not intentional, but it is our job to bring them back, using the stay Mindful skill.

DEAR MAN: APPEAR CONFIDENT: "EYE-CONTACT" = "I-CONTACT" (ME WITH YOU)

As you use your DEAR MAN skills, it is important to appear confident—a big part of which is making eye contact. For a request or a statement to be really effective, it has to be a *person-to-person* statement, and there is nothing more personal than making eye contact.

The universal expression for shame is for one's face and eyes to be downcast. If you do not make eye contact, you are inadvertently telling the other person that you really don't think you deserve what you're asking for. If you do not make eye contact, you are sending the message that not only do you not deserve what you're asking for, you do not deserve to stand in their presence and make the request. The emotional component of the request is just as important as the factual component. Making eye contact is vital to making a person-to-person request. Without it, you are emotionally disconnected from the other person.

DEAR MAN: APPEAR CONFIDENT—STAND UP STRAIGHT, LIKE A CONFIDENT LOBSTER

Psychologist/author Jordan Peterson begins his highly successful book *12 Rules for Life* (Peterson, 2018) with rule 1: "Stand up straight, with your shoulders back." Peterson discusses what scientists have learned about other species, such as chimpanzees and lobsters, including how their posture is a form of communication about their place in their species social hierarchy. A lobster trying to assert itself in the lobster social community will raise up and dance like a boxer, waving its claws back and forth. As two lobsters struggle for dominance in the social hierarchy, they go through a series of rituals to see which is the dominant lobster. Only if a complex series of communications does not establish which is the top dog, do they actually fight. Both the dominant and the subordinated lobster experience neurochemical changes, just like we humans: higher serotonin for the top lobster, and lower serotonin for the down lobster.

In DBT, when we ask for something, or say "no" to what we do not want, we do not want to project the posture of a subordinate lobster. We are not trying to dominate the other person, but neither do we want to put ourselves in an inferior, unworthy light, even when we are in a subordinate position. It is important not to approach others, whether they are our superiors, our peers, or our subordinates with our tail between our legs. I know I am mixing dog and lobster metaphors, but I do so like a confident lobster, without shame. To quote Peterson, I "stand up straight, with my shoulders back." I project confidence. I am worthy and competent. I may even start off feeling a little anxious, but this posture gives me that squirt of serotonin that creates some confidence.

When we stand up straight, with our shoulders back, we are communicating to the other person that we deserve getting what we are asking for. Or at least we deserve to ask for it, without feeling ashamed. By standing up straight, we are communicating to both others and ourselves that we are worthy of our request.

So stand up straight...like a confident lobster!

DEAR MAN: NEGOTIATE SKILL

The Negotiate skill constitutes a surprise to some. Some of us grew up in a family with a "winner take all" mentality, or where there was a fairly rigid line of command, such as a father who was the head of the household, and a mother who did what the father said—there was little room for negotiation between parents and children, etc. Don't get me wrong, parents do need to have the final say in the family, but every relationship contains an element of negotiation.

We know from the study of both unhealthy and healthy relationships that everything is up for negotiation. Having a "winner take all" attitude does not work in the real world. Even when I am in a position of authority over someone (such as an employee, a graduate student I am supervising, or my sons ,ages 13 and 15), I get better results by negotiating. As Marsha Linehan points out, we give in the service of getting. This is what one author termed turning a Win/Lose situation into a Win/Win relationship (a strategy that came out of Harvard Business School.) If we give the other person something they want and this leads to us getting what we want, this is not a losing situation. Some people feel that negotiating with their children is somehow giving up one's power and that this will lead to anarchy in the family. In reality, you are teaching your children the Negotiate skill. You don't give them everything they want, but you do give them something they want *if* they give you what you want.

Experts in the field of relationships point out that healthy couples and families are characterized by negotiation (Gottman & Silver, 1999; Walsh, 2003). It is important that when going for what we want and coming away with only 70 percent, we don't throw a tantrum or storm away from the relationship. Gottman points out in his study of happily married couples that when there is a major conflict between the couple, 69 percent of the time they do not come to a successful resolution of that conflict. Though the happily married couples do not get everything their way over the entire course of the marriage, they still experience their marriage as happy and successful. I believe with the DEAR MAN skills, we ask for what we want, and are willing to take what we can get. Yet I have known people that, if they don't get 100 percent of what they want, they storm away in anger, leaving perhaps 85 percent left on the table. This kind of all-or-nothing thinking is very anti-dialectical.

Perhaps you've had the unrealistic expectation that "I should not have to ask for what I want" or "they should just give in to me." People who are successful in life do not live by this philosophy. They know that life requires negotiation.

GIVE: BE GENTLE—AN IDEA FROM THE BIBLE

One of my favorite quotes from the Bible is when Jesus said to his disciples "be shrewd as snakes, … but harmless as doves" (Matthew 10:16). If you think of it, Jesus is being extremely dialectic, telling his followers to do two things that are very opposite, but both true.

The context of this comment is that Jesus was sending his 12 apostles to nearby communities to spread his message. In the first half of the verse, he uses another metaphor to explain the dangers of this mission: "I am sending you out as sheep in the midst of wolves." The world is like that. While most persons are decent, trustworthy, and benign, there are those who prey upon others financially, sexually, and otherwise (Hare, 1993; Stout, 2003). These wolves manipulate others in the workplace or in social contexts and friendships. There are (as depicted in the teen-comedy film the same name) "mean girls" as well as mean boys. There are sexual predators, scam artists, and persons who portray nicety, but do so to deceive and exploit. There are wolves out there. Some in our culture would prescribe meeting this threat by being an even bigger, badder wolf.

Our culture may tell us that only naïve and gullible people are gentle, that kindness is a by-product of one's weakness and gullibility. To avoid being taken advantage, we must project not only strength, but an aggressive edge—some "swag." But as Jesus's words point out, there is nothing about being gentle that necessitates weakness or gullibility.

In actuality, being gentle is an exercise in shrewdness. Abrasiveness and hostility trigger resistance and opposition. What is so shrewd about that?

GIVE: BE GENTLE—A LESSON FROM BILLIARDS, SET UP YOUR NEXT SHOT

When I was a boy, my family got a pool table. My grandfather had worked in a pool hall in addition to working in an oil refinery. He knew a few things about the game of billiards, which he taught my brothers and me. One thing I remember is him graphically talking about the importance of setting up your next shot. Like most children, I would shoot to put a ball in the pocket, be happy when it went in, but then would often be left with a paucity of shots that anybody short of Minnesota Fats could not possibly make. My grandfather taught me to not only make the shot I was shooting, but to consider where my cue ball was going to end up.

The GIVE skills begin with be **Gentle**. Dr Linehan defines this as no attacking, no threatening, no judging, and no sneering (Linehan, 2015, p. 128). Failing to adhere to this dictum results in damaged and acrimonious relationships. If we fail to be gentle, we may have the very short-term gratification won by "dissing" the other person, perhaps feeling clever with our insult, but then what? We are then left with, metaphorically speaking, "an impossible shot." People who are harsh or abrasive win one battle, but subsequently lose the war.

Being gentle is setting up your next shot. If this is a relationship you want to continue, making sure that the other person feels good about it is crucial.

GIVE—BEING GENTLE DOES NOT MEAN BEING WEAK

A verse in the Bible that always seemed to me quite paradoxical was the passage where Jesus said, "Blessed are the meek, for they shall inherit the earth" (Matthew 5:5). However, this was predicated on my ignorance of what the word "meek" meant in the original (pre-translation) language of the Bible. To me meek meant "weak." However, when one studies this word in the original language (Greek), one finds that it was used by Aristotle to mean a middle path between bad temper and spineless incompetence, between extreme anger and indifference (Bromiley, 1985, p. 930). As such, "meek" means strong, yet non-harmful. Meekness does not equal weakness, but rather an attitude of being gentle while at the same time being strong.

Many today make the same mistake thinking meekness is weakness, so they engage in behaviors that are coarse, with a view to intimidate others and project bravado. Sadly, the overly macho tough-guy or tough girl act is somewhat engrained in our culture.

The question here is: what do you think about being gentle? Do you fear being gentle makes you a target for being taken advantage of? If you are a male, do you fear other people will doubt your masculinity? Regardless of your gender, do you fear that other people will take your gentleness as an open invitation to abuse you?

It is interesting that the passage where Jesus says, "Blessed are the meek, for they shall inherit the earth," as well as the familiar statement about turning the other cheek are both balanced in his famous "Sermon on the Mount" with a statement where he also tells his followers not to throw their pearls before swine, "lest they turn and trample you as well." Notice this is a dialectical understanding of this issue. Jesus is saying there is nothing to be gained by projecting bravado or a "tough guy" persona, nor is there merit in placing ourselves in a position to be passive victims.

I once read a parable of a horrible cobra who would bite many travelers on a road, leaving them sick or even dying. The people of the adjacent town sought a wise man to charm the snake and stop its aggressive actions. The wise man was able to do just that, commanding the cobra to never bite anyone again. Soon people were no longer afraid of the cobra, and it got to the point where the children of the town would taunt the snake, pick it up and drag it, and even throw it for their amusement. One day the wise man was walking down the road and saw the beleaguered cobra, covered with wounds and bruises with a sad expression on his face. "What has happened to you?" the wise man asked. "Since you told me not to bite anyone, people have been taking advantage of me!" replied the cobra. The wise man said, "I told you not to bite anyone, but I did not tell you not to hiss!"

Being gentle doesn't mean being a pushover. It does mean inflicting no emotional harm as a way of getting "one up" on others.

VALIDATE BY NOT INVALIDATING—PEPE LE PEW

One of the Looney Tunes cartoons that I remember as especially creative featured a skunk by the name of Pepe le Pew. In each episode, some unfortunate black cat would somehow accidentally get a stripe of white paint put down her back, making her look like a skunk. Pepe le Pew would mistake her for a female skunk, begin sweet talking with his soft, velvety voice and fancy French accent, put his arms around her and gaze deeply into her eyes, then kissing her arm. Despite all his debonair and sophisticated French charm, about this time the pungent skunk fumes would rise to her nostrils, and the uneasy cat went from being uncomfortable with Pepe's advances to being mortified by the stench.

Pepe le Pew's skunk stench reminds me of invalidation. In a sense it doesn't matter how many validating statements we make, if we make an invalidating remark, it is all for naught. One critical, rejecting, insulting remark can undo many well-meaning actions.

Most of us will make statements that are unintentionally invalidating. The other person's facial expression will tell us of this unintentional invalidation. Once we recognize this, we must respond in deliberate fashion, first communicating that we suspect we have invalidated the other person, then ask them to teach us what it is we did or said that made them feel invalidated. Do not, and again I repeat *do not* try to explain away your behavior or words. Your job is not to be your own defense attorney and somehow acquit yourself of any wrong doing *if* you want to repair the relationship. If you make the case that what you said was not wrong or harmful, you are invalidating the person even more, throwing salt into their wounds. Your role at this point is to understand what it was that was so invalidating to them. You ask them to be the teacher, and your role is to be the student. While it is usually true that the invalidating statement or action was not intentional, it is a fatal mistake to assert that this means that it was no big deal. Only after you fully understand what it was like to be the other person, should you convey that invalidating them was not your intent, *but do not deny your action, nor how it made them feel.*

After the other person teaches you why the remark was hurtful, your next step is also crucial. The next step is to simply sit with what they have told you. This is the opposite of saying, "yes, but ..." Let yourself chew on what they have said. You can ask more questions to help you understand it more fully. Remember, Marsha Linehan teaches us that understanding the other person's point of view and their feelings does not mean that we agree with all of their viewpoint. It does mean that we respect their belief and emotions, and we do not assume the attitude that they are stupid or wrong for looking at things differently than we do. If we do respect them, we will take time to ponder what they have told us rather than quickly dismissing it.

Remember, a skunk by any other name smells just as bad. No amount of perfume is a substitute for getting rid of our invalidating and judgmental attitude and communication.

VALIDATE WITH YOUR WHOLE WISE MIND

To validate somebody else, we have to understand them not only on an intellectual level, but on an emotional one as well. As such, we need to understand others with our Wise Mind, using both our intellect and our emotions (Reasonable Mind and Emotion Mind respectively).

My first academic and professional pursuit was not in psychology, but in theology, culminating in me being ordained as a minister. I was ordained in a church that did not ordain women. Positions of leadership were exclusively for men.

I did some post-graduate training in something called Clinical Pastoral Education or "CPE." It was here that, for the first time, I met people who worked in ministry who were women. One of our teachers was a fairly progressive nun, Sister Barbara. One day, our educational task included a role play, directed by Sister Barbara, in which she said we were going to pretend we were having a cocktail party. We were to invent and play a character who was of the opposite sex. I became Linda, and I was a nurse. As we mingled about and talked to other people, I met Sister Barbara's character whose name was John. "John" asked "what kind of job do you have, Linda?" "I am a nurse." "That's a nice job... for a woman." Suddenly I felt blind rage and the urge to choke the everlasting shit out of "John" (Sister Barbara). Only at this point did I begin to have a fully Wise-Minded view of what it must be like to be a woman, especially in the early 1980s in the Midwest.

To validate somebody else, we first have to put ourselves into the shoes of the other person and understand them both intellectually and emotionally. Remember, you may not agree with their point of view, but you will need to understand it *and feel it* to implement this skill.

GIVE: ACT INTERESTED SKILL

When Marsha Linehan tells us to "act Interested," is she telling us to fake our emotions? I would say "no;" I think she is telling us to *invest* our emotions.

Years ago, I went with two friends for vacation to the city of Chicago. We were unwinding in our hotel room at the end of the day. One of these friends had started his own whole-grain bakery, more as a labor of love than a get-rich-quick scheme. He was lying in bed, reading a book, with a huge grin on his face. Curious, I shifted around to see the title the book. What was the fascinating tome that so captivated my friend? Answer: *The Yeasts of Great Britain*. I did not find different strains of yeasts to be a fascinating subject, but because it fascinated my friend, it was (somewhat) interesting to me.

If we are truly interested in another person, this includes being interested in what they are interested in. We allow ourselves to become interested in their world because it is important to them. A hallmark of psychological maturity is the ability to invest in someone else, not being limited to our individual preferences.

The other part of what "act Interested" means we make sure we communicate our interest non-verbally, letting our interest be broadcasted by our facial expression, body language, and tone of voice. When I do couples or family therapy, I sometimes see one person with very little eye contact or facial expression when the other one talks. I check in with the poker-face person to see what's going on with them. Sometimes they are very interested in what their family member is saying, but they have been taught to be emotionally non-expressive. Their loved one thinks they aren't really listening or interested, but they are! *Acting Interested* means being *unambiguous* that we are paying attention, and that the other person's thoughts and feelings are important to us.

If you want to care for and cultivate a relationship, act interested!

RELATIONSHIP EFFECTIVENESS: VALIDATE SKILL

When teaching the Validate skill, I point out the similarity to the word *value* which comes from the same Latin root. When we invalidate another person's feelings or ideas we are saying that a significant part of who they are has no value. We are not just saying their opinion is worthless, we are, in effect, saying *they are worthless*. Do you see how invalidating someone else can kill a relationship?

Every time we have an interaction with another person, we have the opportunity to strengthen the relationship… or damage to the relationship. Do you value that other person? Every statement you make is potentially a validating one. At minimum, you want to be mindful to not damage the relationship with an invalidating comment.

If you are in a DBT group, it is likely that you have been harmed by, at minimum, a fair amount invalidation. This is your opportunity to rise far above where you came from, and live your life on the higher plane of Relationship Effectiveness by validating others, even when they are different.

EASY MANNER SKILL: GOLDILOCKS AND THE THREE BEARS

Goldilocks and the Three Bears is a children's' story familiar to everyone in Western civilization. I find it curious how no one holds Goldilocks accountable for Breaking and Entering the home of the three bears (a felony in most jurisdictions). Goldilocks gets into the three bears' house and, hungry, begins to sample the porridge of the three bears. Papa Bear's porridge is too hot, Mama Bear's is too cold, and Baby Bear's is "just right."

Many people do not realize that this story is a metaphor that applies to almost every situation in life. We can err not only too far to the left, but too far to the right. When it comes to being effective in maintaining and strengthening a relationship, we can be either too serious, or too cavalier and jocular. With the Easy Manner skill the use of *some* humor sends the message that we are not taking ourselves or the situation too seriously; it sends the signal to the other person that we are not taking "a superior attitude" in which we are trying to control the other person. Easy Manner signals that we have no intention of playing a winner-take-all approach, or that we will inflict judgment if things don't go our way. An Easy Manner signals to the other party that we are flexible and gentle. It signals to the other person that they don't have to be on guard, on high alert status. As such, it is indispensable for Relationship Effectiveness.

SELF-RESPECT EFFECTIVENESS—A LESSON FROM JOAN JETT

It is not enough to get our objective met or to have a solid relationship. We must also preserve our self-respect and dignity, otherwise we are paying too high a price for having a relationship. Many people sacrifice their self-respect for the sake of having a relationship, and are a prisoner of dissatisfaction.

A song illustrates this point: "I Hate Myself for Loving You," recorded by Joan Jett and the Blackhearts (Child & Jett, 1988), tells just such a story. A person is stood up by their date and experiences hurt and social humiliation. Many persons get mistreated and abused by a partner repeatedly, yet so fear losing the relationship that they continue to endure the heartache, humiliation, and harm to their psyche (and unfortunately sometimes to their body).

DBT teaches us that our self-respect is just as important as having a relationship or getting what we want from someone. This is where the FAST skills come in. The first is **Be Fair** to yourself and others. I vividly remember one group member who watched me put this on the board and exclaimed, "That's my problem, I'm always fair to other people, but not to myself!"

It is true that Marsha Linehan tells us that sometimes we do sacrifice a little bit of one of the three objectives (Objective, Relationship, or Self-respect Effectiveness) to gain in the other two. To use my metaphor of the three-legged stool that illustrates the three goals of Interpersonal Effectiveness, we can saw off a couple inches of one of the legs, and the stool will still stand. I have endured petty insults and disrespectful environments to accomplish my goals, but when the abusive treatment begins to have a negative impact on my self-respect, it is time to assert my need to be treated fairly. Our heart will tell us if we are not being fair to ourselves or to the other person. If our heart says, "I hate myself for loving you," we need to make a change. Either we stand up for being treated fairly, or we need to let go of a hopeless relationship.

"I hate myself for loving you" … a great song, … but a lousy, ineffective way to live.

FAST SKILL: S = STICK TO YOUR VALUES TO MAINTAIN SELF-RESPECT EFFECTIVENESS

The worst vacation I ever went on was to one of the coolest places on the planet, Memphis, Tennessee. I saw the famed Sun Studio where rock and roll was invented by Elvis Presley,

Carl Perkins, Johnny Cash, and Jerry Lee Lewis. I greatly enjoyed seeing Elvis's Mansion, Graceland. People were wonderful, the food was delicious, and blues music on Beale Street was awesome. So why was this a vacation from hell?

On this vacation, I was pressured to compromise my values, and I gave in and did so. As such, I felt horrible throughout the entire experience. I was not as assertive at that time in my life (many decades ago), and so I kept just trying to just get along. I sacrificed my self-respect to maintain the relationship, and had one of the most dreadful experiences of my life. Early on in the trip, we were eating at an excellent restaurant in Memphis, which is famous for its barbecued ribs. The waiter brought a check, and my travel companions quickly recognized that it was the wrong check. They said, "Look, it's for only two people" (there were four of us), and quickly money came out to pay the bill before the staff figured out the mistake. I did not see this coming, and, stunned and facing social pressure, I just drifted along.

Several days later we were taking our vehicle out of the hotel parking garage, and nobody brought their room key so that our parking could be validated. When the parking attendant said we needed to either go get a key or pay for our parking, my friends started getting nasty, hostile, and perhaps even menacing. I was appalled, but did not stick to my values. I wanted to say "Hey, she is just doing her job," but didn't. The intimidated parking attendant said she would call her manager to resolve the situation, and my friends thought they had attained a great victory. Sixty seconds later, a police car with lights flashing pulled in behind us and the officer asked what the problem was. After we paid and left, my travel companions railed against how uncool the parking attendant was. I thought we got exactly what we had asked for, but was outnumbered three to one. I did not **stick to my values.**

The point of this story is that I was in one of the coolest places on earth, and yet because I did not stick to my values in the relationship, I felt awful for the entire trip. I completely surrendered my self-respect.

As a post-script to this unfortunate trip: once back in Cincinnati I located the address of the restaurant, and sent the amount of money that I calculated we probably skipped out on. I sent it with an explanation, describing what our waiter looked like, knowing he probably got stuck with the shortfall. That restored *some* of my self-respect. But I wish I had been proactive with the FAST skill of *Stick to your Values*.

FAST: BE TRUTHFUL, AN EXAMPLE FROM HISTORY

The final of the FAST skills, be **Truthful** is important to maintaining and strengthening one's self-dignity. Several examples below will illustrate this.

Senator Joseph McCarthy was an ambitious young politician who had a track record of not telling the truth before he was elected to the Senate from the state of Wisconsin in 1947 (Tye, 2020). For example, when he enlisted in the Marine Corps for service in World War II, he was assigned to be a tail gunner for a bomber in the Pacific. There he flew and fought in 12 missions, then was discharged. Later, when running for office, he claimed he flew 32 missions. When he was running against an incumbent judge who was 66 years old, McCarthy claimed his opponent was 73 years old.

After being elected to the US Senate in 1947, McCarthy served for three years, had a low-key manner, and somewhat unremarkable record. This all changed on February 9, 1951; McCarthy was making a speech to the women's Republican Club of Wheeling, West Virginia. He held up a piece of paper and claimed that he had a list of communists who had infiltrated the U.S. State Department, asserting this put our freedom in grave peril. Historians cannot determine the number of supposed communists on this list—some witnesses said it was 205 whereas other said it was 57. What we do know was this claim was picked up by newspapers and went viral. Suddenly, people from coast to coast knew who Joseph McCarthy was. He attained instant fame as an anti-communist hero, protecting America from our greatest danger.

There was just one problem with McCarthy's sudden fame and fortune; he completely made up the allegation of all these supposed communists. From 1951 on, McCarthy continued to claim that he had information on communist infiltrators in the State Department, the administration of President Harry S. Truman, the United States Army, and many in Hollywood. Lives and careers were destroyed.

However, by 1953 and 1954 people began to wise up to what McCarthy was doing. On December 2, 1950, the Senate censured McCarthy for his antics by a vote of 67 to 22. After this condemnation, McCarthy was disgraced, with most Americans viewing him not as a hero but as an opportunist and a man who had no allegiance to the truth. He became the proverbial boy who cried wolf. No one in the Senate paid much attention to him, and his speeches on the floor of the Senate were attended by a few, with many of these not really paying much attention. McCarthy had always been a heavy drinker, but now disgraced, he began to drink more heavily and colleagues said that they saw him drunk on the Senate floor.

McCarthy's downfall was that he let his ambition eclipse his commitment to truth. His objective was to become famous, persuasive, and to achieve high status in the eyes of America. He fell into complete disgrace in his efforts to achieve this objective. No doubt, the shame he incurred fueled his alcoholism and led to his untimely death at age 48.

When we sacrifice our commitment to being *truthful*, we sacrifice our dignity. Be Truthful—it will maintain your self-respect and the respect of others.

FAST: BE TRUTHFUL, A COUNTER-INTUITIVE SKILL

Being truthful can pay benefits that are part of the values-based, mindful approach to life that DBT teaches. When teaching a graduate school course on Professional Ethics, I came across a study that I found intriguing and perhaps counterintuitive. Researchers Gerald Koocher and Patricia Keith-Spiegel (2008) studied malpractice lawsuits in the practice of medicine and found a very important piece of information. Physicians who readily admitted to patients and their families that they had made a mistake were much less likely to be sued for malpractice than physicians who covered up and lied about their mistakes. Physicians who attempted to cover up their mistakes were much more likely to be sued for malpractice.

We may be tempted to conceal or distort truth for the sake of preserving a relationship or attaining an objective, but the price we pay in lost dignity and respect is potentially very high.

REFERENCES

Bromiley, G W. (1985) *Theological dictionary of the New Testament: Abridged in one volume.* (Kittel, G. & Friedrich, G. editors). Grand Rapids: William B. Eerdmans.

Carnegie, D. (1998) *How to win friends & influence people.* New York, NY, US: Simon & Schuster.

Child, D & Jett, J. (1988) *I hate myself for loving you.* On Up Your Alley [record]. Germany: Polydor.

Gottman, J M & Silver, N. (1999) *The seven principles for making marriage work.* New York: Three Rivers Press.

Hare, R D. (1993) *Without a conscience: the disturbing world of the psychopaths among us.* New York, Guilford Press.

Jacquet, L. (2005) *March of the Penguins.* National Geographic Films.

Koocher, G P & Keith-Spiegel, P. (2008) *Ethics in psychology and the mental health professions: Standards and cases* (3rd ed.). New York, NY, US: Oxford University Press.

Linehan, M M. (2015) *DBT skills training: Handouts and worksheets.* New York: Guilford.

Miller, W R, editor. (1999) *Integrating spirituality into treatment: Resources for practitioners.* Washington: American Psychological Association.

Miller, W R & Rollnick. (2013). Motivational interviewing: Helping *people change*, third Edition. New York: Guilford.

Peterson, J B. (2018) *12 rules for life: An antidote to chaos.* Penguin Books. Westminster

Pink, D H. (2009) Drive: *The surprising truth about what motivates us.* New York, NY, US: Penguin Group Inc.

Richards, P S & Bergin, A E. (2005) *A spiritual strategy for counseling and psychotherapy: Second Edition.* Washington, American Psychological Association.

Stout, M. (2005) *The sociopath next door.* Harmony Books.

Tye, L. (2020) *Demagogue: The life and long shadow of Senator Joe McCarthy.* Boston, Houghton Mifflin Harcourt.

Walsh, F. (2003) *Normal family processes: Growing diversity and complexity.* New York: Guilford Press.

Emotion Regulation

Chapter 4

EMOTION REGULATION—WHAT IS REGULATION?
METAPHOR: A CITY WITHOUT TRAFFIC LIGHTS

Imagine what would happen if the traffic lights of a city suddenly disappeared. There would be sudden chaos, auto accidents, and traffic jams galore.

What do traffic lights do? Answer: they *regulate* traffic. Regulated traffic flows efficiently, allowing everyone to get where they are going, with no one getting harmed. Emotions are like traffic; when they are regulated, they help us get things done, live enjoyable and satisfying lives, and live in harmony with others. Without regulation, our lives become a cluster of gridlock, painful collisions, and road rage. Neither traffic nor emotions are bad, but if neither are regulated, we incur frustration and aggravation galore. You are not to blame for the fact that the city planners did not install enough traffic lights in the city of your life, however it is now your responsibility to install what you need. Welcome to the Emotion Regulation module.

As you begin the Emotion Regulation module, think of each new skill as a traffic light that will bring organization and "happy traveling" to your life.

WHY REGULATE EMOTIONS? WALKING THE DOG

Nine years ago my family got a dog, a wonderful dog—half Golden Retriever, half English Bloodhound. We named him Cubby, after one of our favorite baseball teams, the Chicago Cubs. Our boys were only four and six, and Cubby was a big and powerful dog. At six feet tall and 200 pounds, I had trouble guiding this powerful pup on the leash. My sons wanted to take their turn on the leash. At best, they held on and Cubby ran wherever he wanted until my wife or I could catch up and regain control. At worst, Cub would jerk the leash out their hands and might be on the loose for 30 minutes or more. Cubby out of our control was real trouble. He could run out in traffic and be hit by a motor vehicle and die. He could chase a cat or tangle with another dog. He could get away from us, lose his way, and we might never see him again.

As Cubby got older, we trained him to work *with* us rather than simply having a mind of his own. If he wanted to stop and smell an object, or even backtrack to smell something, we would let him. But though the dog's desires are not bad, ultimately the owner needs to be in control, and, sometimes completely override the will of the dog.

Think of your emotions as your dog. You want the best for your dog, you want your dog to be happy, but ultimately do you walk your dog, or does your dog walk you? Who is in control? If you feel your emotions are dragging you around, getting you into situations you regret, the emotion regulation module can be like obedience training for an unruly dog. The goal is not to beat the dog into submission, nor eliminate its spontaneity or its unique personality. The goal is for you and your dog to have an enjoyable experience together. A dog who is well regulated by its master is a happy dog indeed.

The Emotion Regulation module will be your dog trainer. You will learn how to understand the needs of your emotions and the value of what they are signaling to you. And yet you will be the master, and your Wise Mind will know when to reign in the impulses of your Emotion Mind. Both dog and owner will be much more satisfied when the two of you graduate from this sort of "obedience school."

REGULATING EMOTIONS: GOLDILOCKS AND THE THREE BEARS

Often, when overwhelmed by our emotions, the problem is not the emotion itself, but the intensity of the emotion (Linehan,

2015a, p. 231.) As I state elsewhere in this book, we can have a $ 200 reaction to a $5 problem. Other individuals will make us mad, final exams and demands at work can make us anxious, treating someone badly or letting them down can make us feel guilty. If our anger prompts us to speak up and tell our friends we don't like one of their actions, it has served its rightful purpose, but if the intensity of our anger over a small to medium-sized issue turns into rage, it destroys our friendships. If our fear of an exam energizes us to study diligently, it serves its purpose. But if the level of anxiety created by the exam is too intense, it can paralyzes us, so that study is impossible, and we fail. If our sense of guilt pains us to the point of not repeating a harmful behavior, it makes us a better person. If the sense of guilt immobilizes us with depression and self-hatred, it no longer serves an adaptive purpose for our behavior.

I often invoke the story of the Goldilocks and the Three Bears. Goldilocks invades the bears' house, is hungry, and tries some of Papa Bear's porridge, which is too hot, whereas Mama Bear's porridge is too cold and Baby Bear's is just right. For years, I dismissed this as a childish story, but as I became older I realized the wisdom within this ancient fable. Most situations call for us to avoid too much or too little, to find where "just right" is.

If you are in a DBT group, it is likely that your emotions have tended to run "too hot." But there are also times when our emotions run too cold. More than once, college students, failing most or all of their courses, have been referred to me for counseling. In the cases where the student does little homework during the bulk of the semester, I explore whether at the beginning of the next semester if receiving their syllabus provokes anxiety. The answer is often "no." I point out that it would be helpful to experience a small to medium amount of anxiety, because this can energize us to begin working on assignments, rather than wait until the last minute.

Emotions are not bad. But if they are "too hot," we react impulsively—our behavioral response does not fit the situation. If our emotions are "too cold," we don't have the motivation we need to do what we need to do.

The Emotion Regulation module will get you to "just right."

FIRST GOAL OF EMOTION REGULATION— UNDERSTAND YOUR EMOTIONS

Emotions happen in reaction to prompting events. However, other factors contribute to the actual content of the emotion that emerges. For example, consider the situation of a teacher asking a student to answer a question in class. This may elicit happiness in one student; her *interpretation* is the teacher called on her because she has confidence in her knowledge, and the student feels validated. Another student may react with fear because he has not studied and does not know the answer, or perhaps a *vulnerability factor* is in play; the person may have a learning disability and a history of being shamed for not answering correctly.

Here is another example: a man and a woman are on a date, and one begins to ask for or initiate some degree of physical intimacy. The other may feel happiness that their date is attracted to them. Perhaps the feelings are mutual and the recipient of this advance is experiencing some degree of romantic love. However, if this is too quick for this person's sensibilities, or if they are not attracted to the date in similar fashion, the person may feel anxiety and/or a small degree of disgust, signaling this advance is not accepted. Lastly, if the recipient of the advance has incurred trauma (a *vulnerability factor*) they may react with a feeling of fear, shame, and/or disgust. It could be that *interpretation* plays a major role in the person's emotional reaction. He or she may believe that the other is moving too quickly and that they are being seen as "easy," and thus may become furious with this behavior. The important thing for this person to do is pay attention to their feelings and interpretation and vulnerability factors, understanding their emotion as a response to all three.

The first goal of the Emotion Regulation module is to **understand our emotions**. My belief is that Marsha Linehan deliberately listed this as the *first* goal. Before we try to change emotions, we need to understand them, because understanding our emotions is the essence of understanding ourselves. If we try to change an unpleasant emotion without understanding it, we run the risk of invalidating ourselves.

THE SECOND, THIRD, AND FOURTH GOALS OF THE EMOTION REGULATION MODULE

After the first goal of the Emotion Regulation (ER) module (understand our emotions), Dr Linehan suggests that we "**decrease the *frequency* of *unwanted* emotions**". She chose this phrase very wisely. Note that she did not say "make bad emotions never happen."

First of all, no emotions are "bad." They can be unpleasant and painful, but they are there for a purpose. When I was in graduate school, we listed the primary emotions universal to all humans on the board. They are the same ones listed on pages 214–222 of the *DBT Skills Training Handouts and Worksheets, Second Edition* (anger, disgust, envy, fear, jealousy, sadness, shame, guilt, happiness, and love) plus several others including boredom and loneliness. If you count the number of unpleasant to pleasant possible emotional states, that comes to ten unpleasant and two pleasant emotions. My immediate reaction to seeing this was "wow, life sucks!"

But years later I made more sense of what this configuration of emotional experience really means. The ten unpleasant emotions are telling us to change something. Anger tells us to assert ourselves, by asserting what we want, or saying "no!" to what we do not want. Fear tells us to get away from danger. Guilt tells us we have damaged a relationship, to make sure we don't do it again, and make restitution if possible. Boredom tells us we need something more interesting, and loneliness tells us we need to seek more human contact. Happiness and love tell us we are exactly where we need to be.

We want to reduce the frequency of unwanted emotions. Periodic experience of painful emotions will happen, but DBT teaches us to prevent these emotions as much as possible by realizing (in most cases) it is a cue to change something. We now see the unpleasant emotion as a signal—loneliness = "I need more friends"—and we can respond to the signal.

The third goal of the ER module is **decrease emotional vulnerability**. Certain things will make us more vulnerable. Not having an adequate amount of sleep will turn any of us into a grouch, in a bad mood for the rest of the day. So will a hangover. So will having unstable blood sugar.

This module emphasizes setting ourselves up for having a good mood day by preventing things that will start us off in a bad mood (see the PLEASE skills later in this chapter.)

Fourthly, the ER module helps us to **decrease emotional suffering**. All of us will have emotional pain, but suffering comes when we hold onto the pain, often by holding onto grudges and other judgmental thoughts. Frequently, we expand our suffering by telling ourselves "this bad thing should not have happened!" Although it is not part of the ER module per se, the Radical Acceptance skills (in the Distress Tolerance module) are very helpful in preventing added suffering.

EMOTION REGULATION—WHAT GOOD ARE EMOTIONS? METAPHORS: "DON'T KILL THE MESSENGER" AND "SPRAY-PAINTING THE INSTRUMENT PANEL"

Patients sometimes tell me "I hate feeling that emotion!" Trouble comes when we take shortcuts to get relief from the pain of the emotion, such as abusing substances, self-harm, compulsive shopping, etc. When we do this, we are, in effect, killing the messenger (i.e., emotions), and ignoring the message. The problem persists, and our Emotion Mind will keep sending the messengers until the underlying problem is resolved.

Take loneliness as an example. Although no one wants to feel this, loneliness is a messenger, telling you that you need more human contact. Loneliness is not a "symptom," it is your "friend," telling you what you need.

Imagine someone, annoyed by an "oil needed" message on the dashboard of their car, responding by spray painting over the symbol? Ludicrous? But sometimes we also try to paint over our painful emotions with abuse of drugs or other destructive behaviors, rather than trying to understand what the emotions are telling us.

No one may have ever helped you understand how to understand your emotions and that is not your fault. Fortunately, your DBT therapist and DBT skills group will help you read your instrument panel and know what in-flight corrections to make.

EMOTION REGULATION—BENEFITS INCLUDE SOCIAL COMPETENCE AND RESILIENCE

There is real value into digging into the name of this module and fully understanding it. Regulation means to control. When explaining this to my DBT group, I draw a thermostat on the dry-erase board and we talk about how this is used to regulate the temperature in a room. If it is too hot, we cool it down. If it is too cold, we warm it up.

Psychological research points out that persons with optimal Emotion Regulation are neither over-controlled nor under-controlled (Gross, 2007, p. 295; Lynch, 2018). Persons who neither over-control or under-control their emotions tend to be the best adjusted, the most socially competent and most resilient when faced with adversity. This jives with common sense: persons who are emotionally volatile are not well-liked. Persons who have extreme emotional reactions get put down more quickly in life's journey. Persons who are overcontrolled are seen as "uptight," not fun to be around, and as not enjoying life very much.

DECREASING EMOTIONAL SENSITIVITY AND INTENSITY—A $200 REACTION TO A $5 PROBLEM

"It's like you had a $200 reaction to a $5 problem." "That's it exactly!" Over and over again I have had this conversation with dozens of clients in the last ten to 15 years.

The first edition of the DBT skills training manual (Linehan, 1993b) listed decreasing emotional sensitivity as one of the goals of the ER module. The $200 reaction to the $5 problem metaphor illustrates how our emotions are valid, but the volume/intensity of the reaction is over-amplified, making the intensity of our emotion too high for us to respond effectively to the problem.

Automobiles have shock absorbers. In a perfect world, no roads would have potholes or bumps, but we do not live in a perfect world. Shock absorbers absorb the impact from holes. If we are more emotionally sensitive than most people, the ER Module can help us acquire shock absorbers and become less vulnerable to the bumps in the road of life. If someone says something insulting or snarky, feeling angry or hurt is a normal response, but our shock absorbers will prevent us from being completely devastated.

Imagine if you lost all the pain receptors in your hands—in a short amount of time, you would have all sorts of cuts and burns. Likewise, our emotional pain receptors are there to tell us what is harmful. But we do not want to have a $200 response to a $5 problem. The Emotion Regulation module will help you to have $5 reactions to $5 problems, $100 reactions to $100 problems, etc. This module will give you emotional shock absorbers. Hitting a big pothole will not be pleasant, but you will not have your teeth jarred out. Small waves may rock your boat a bit, but they won't flip it over.

DECREASING EMOTIONAL SENSITIVITY

An allergy occurs when our immune system reacts to something as if it were a threat to our health when, in fact, it is not. Tree pollen does not really pose any danger to my well-being, but my immune system reacts to it like a potentially lethal toxin. My immune system *thinks* tree pollen is the devil himself, and attacks it with fury. The result: I get a runny nose and watery eyes. I take several medications to decrease my system's over-reactivity to seasonal pollens and to regulate my immune system's reaction.

If you are studying DBT, it is likely certain things trigger an emotional overreaction, one that is painful and renders you less able to formulate an effective response to your situation. The things that overwhelm you probably do not bother other people to the same degree. Wouldn't it be great if you could just take a Claritin every day and trust that it would prevent such overreactions to things other people say or do?

The DBT Emotion Regulation module is in some ways the antihistamine that will make your life much more tolerable, allowing you to enjoy life. Just like an antihistamine, you just have to make sure that you use the skills every day.

EMOTIONS COMMUNICATE TO OTHERS

It is a myth that Emotion Mind is completely unwise. However, without Reasonable Mind as its partner, Emotion Mind has many blind spots that can lead to unwise decisions and behaviors. However, it is also true that Emotion Mind brings to the table its own wisdom. Without Emotion Mind, Reasonable Mind (by itself) is impoverished, and just as unwise.

Eighteen years ago, I went to my primary care physician for my annual physical. I did the labs ahead of time. He greeted me, and had me step up on the scale. I was surprised how heavy I became. I weighed 252 pounds. Dr Hellman's eyes looked a little concerned. Dr Hellman then opened the manila folder that held my chart. Now his eyes became really big. Alarmed he said, "your blood pressure is up...your cholesterol is up... your triglycerides are up..." he then looked up from the chart and into my eyes, "You are in trouble." I was scared shitless.

Over the next several months, I lost close to 30 pounds. Since then I have dropped under 200 pounds. Dr Hellman communicated very directly to me that day. He communicated the facts (Reasonable Mind) and his emotion, which was *fear* for my well-being (Emotion Mind). Because Dr Hellman communicated both, it was a "Wise Mind message." Without Emotion Mind (as well as Reasonable Mind) communication from Dr Hellman, I would not have turned my life around. I needed the emotional message of fear to move me into sustained action. One of the purposes of emotion is it motivates—it *moves us* to action.

PURPOSE OF EMOTION—EMOTION COMMUNICATES TO OTHERS

When my brother married his wife, he also welcomed her five-year-old son Jamie, and a new family was formed. I liked Jamie, he was (and is) a wonderful nephew, bright, friendly, curious, and thoughtful. Jamie always got along with everyone in the Esmail family, and I always enjoyed seeing him, talking to him, and throwing the football with him. But I always wondered, how much did Jamie feel like an Esmail? How emotionally connected to us as a family was he? Could it be that Jamie was just a friendly and good-natured kid with everyone? Was he simply doing what friendly good-natured kids do?

Our father died when Jamie was about 12 years old. When Jamie came to the hospice center where "Grandpa Jack" passed away, he, of all people, was the most visibly distraught. Jamie, by far, had the most outward expression of grief (tears, red eyes) of anyone. This reminded me of a passage in the Bible, where Jesus' friend Lazarus dies. The gospel of John tells us that "Jesus wept," and observers remarked, "Behold how he loved him!"

Emotion communicates to others. On that day, Jamie's emotions told me more about him than an hour of intellectual verbiage could. Jamie *loved* Grandpa Jack.

PURPOSE OF EMOTION—EMOTION *MOTIVATES* US

Notice that the word e<u>mot</u>ion looks like other words, such as <u>mot</u>ivate and loco<u>mot</u>ive. The Latin root word, mot, means to move. That is why emotion exists, to *move* us. Have you ever said, "I just can't get motivated"? What you are really saying is "I am not experiencing enough emotion to get *moving*" with the necessary behavior to accomplish your goal.

Have you ever wondered why in sports the home team has the advantage? (I ask this question frequently in DBT skills groups and other contexts; I am surprised how many people don't know the answer). The home team receives energy from its fans, who cheer for them. As the fans cheer and the athletes hear it, the athletes' emotion mind receives this energy, which is converted to physical energy as it signals their body to create more adrenalin. As a result, the athletes become "fired up."

I had a similar experience on a whitewater rafting trip 25 years ago. We were on the New River in West Virginia, and stopped for a break. Our guide told us that the next section of the river was the most dangerous, that several people had been killed there. This section of the river had been dubbed "the meat grinder." A friend asked me if I wanted to take a turn being in the very front of the raft, and I accepted.

As soon as we hit the rapids, a large wave of water came and lifted me out of the raft, and I was adrift in the most dangerous part of the river. Within seconds I was carried perhaps 20 feet away from the raft. The guide threw the rescue rope to me, but I was already too far away. I tried to swim towards the rope, but the best I could do was prevent myself from getting even farther away. She stood up and began screaming "swim! SWIM! SWIM#$%@A&*!" What I heard at this point was not only her words, but her emotion. I heard sheer terror in her voice. My response to this emotion was that I, too, felt a rush of terror, followed by a huge rush of adrenalin. The adrenalin gave me the physical strength to swim against the current. I was able to reach the rope and be pulled to safety.

Therapists frequently encourage patients to get in touch with their feelings in the "here and now" of the session. If the patient is to make a positive behavior change, they must garner enough emotion to power the change (Wampold & Imel 2015, p. 48, Yalom & Leszcz, 2005, p. 536; Greenberg & Paivio, 1997, p. 9; Beck, 2011, p. 142).

One of the things I found so refreshing when DBT came out was that, contrary to more traditional therapies at the time, Marsha Linehan not only allowed but promoted therapists to be cheerleaders for behavioral change (Linehan, 1993a, pp. 242–246). We change our lives by changing behavior, but that behavior change is often difficult. We need the "home-field advantage" that comes with people who cheer for us. Emotion is needed to move us into successful change.

PURPOSE OF EMOTION—EMOTION *MOTIVATES* US— METAPHOR—STEAM LOCOMOTIVE

Previously I pointed out that the word emotion looks like other words, such as *motivate* and *locomotive*. When teaching DBT skills groups, I often draw a picture of a steam locomotive and discuss the origin of the word. The Latin root word means to move, and the locomotive is the part of the train that moves (usually by pulling) the train. Without the locomotive, a collection of railroad cars would never move, it would just sit there on the tracks.

Without our emotions, we can do nothing, just like a train without a locomotive. One must have Emotion Mind in the mix to be in Wise Mind. A train with no locomotive would not be very wise, would it? If we extend this metaphor, Reasonable Mind could be the tracks, keeping the train from running amuck, and Wise Mind could be the engineer. But without the locomotive, the train will go nowhere.

My long-time guitar teacher, Craig Wilson, once shared a pearl of wisdom: "half of my job is teaching my students how to play correctly, the other half is **motivating** them to practice."

If you have seen inside an old steam locomotive in action, you saw not one, but two people running the locomotive. One was the engineer (who drives the train), the other is the fireman whose job is to continually build the fire that creates the steam that pushes the engine's pistons. I frequently encourage patients to get in touch with their feelings in the "here and now" of the session, knowing that if meaningful behavior change is going to happen, it will be emotion that powers this change. At this moment during a session, I am more of a fireman (stoking the fire within) than the engineer.

Previously, I spoke of how, in sports, the emotion of the fans creates "the home-field advantage." One of the things I found so refreshing when DBT was introduced to the professional community is that (compared with older, more traditional therapies), Marsha Linehan not only allowed, but *promoted* therapists to be cheerleaders for behavioral change (Linehan, 1993a, pp. 242–246). DBT allows therapists to be the fireman, feeding the fire within you, the cheerleader, rooting you on the victory of behavioral change leading to a life worth living.

WHAT GOOD ARE EMOTIONS? COMMUNICATE TO OURSELVES—METAPHOR—COCKPIT OF AN AIRPLANE

Imagine the cockpit of an airplane. The cockpit is filled gauges and dials which communicate vital information about the airplane's speed, pitch, altitude, as well as information about the airspace around the plane. I read an article about the tragic death of John F Kennedy Jr., who was flying a single prop plane that crashed in foggy weather. JFK, Jr. had not been fully trained and certified to fly with "instruments only" in zero visibility weather. He was unable to rely solely on what his gauges told him. Without visual input, he lost his orientation and crashed, resulting in his untimely death.

Our emotions (love, happiness, fear, loneliness, sadness, jealousy, etc.) are the gauges and dials in our cockpit. Each emotion tells us something about the relationship of our plane to the environment we are flying in.

Much of Emotion Regulation is about learning to read and understand your gauges (emotions). Of course, you also need to know what to do in response to what the gauges are telling you (specific skills you will learn in the Emotion Regulation module).

When doing individual, couples, or family therapy, I often asked people "what are you feeling right now?" I am not doing this to mimic a cheesy TV therapist, I am checking to see if they know how to read their gauges. The same is true for reading the gauges of their loved one in the session. Perhaps they do know how to read the gauges, but are not paying attention to them in that moment.

What good are emotions? Answer: they communicate to us. The Emotion Regulation module will help you to avoid "flying blind."

DESCRIBING YOUR EMOTIONS—YOU MAY NOT BE AS COMPETENT AS YOU THINK, AT LEAST NOT *YET*

Being able to identify and correctly label our emotions is one of the most important life skills any of us will learn. (Want to learn more? read the book *Raising an Emotionally Intelligent Child* [Gottman, 1997]).

In therapy, I work with some very intelligent people: physicians, research scientists, business leaders, and educators. And yet these intelligent people, and even other mental health professionals I work with, are often not good at identifying their own emotions. When I asked one of these intelligent people what they are feeling, they may tell me "upset." This is like being asked "where are you?" and answering, "In the Western Hemisphere." Saying one is "upset" is true, and it does narrow down the scope of possibilities—I know they are not happy—but I still do not know whether they are afraid, terrified, sad, ashamed, angry, frustrated, lonely, disgusted…. afraid is very different from frustrated, which is very different from ashamed.

Another thing that happens when I ask intelligent persons about their emotions is they talk about all sorts of aspects of the situation prompting the emotion, *but ignore describing the emotion itself*. For example, if I ask someone how they feel about their child's use of illegal drugs, they will talk about the health and legal risks involved, reasons why their child should not use the substances, ask where did they get the drugs, etc. They talk *around* the emotion without actually naming the emotion. In this example, only when I am able to get the parent to say "I'm afraid, I'm very scared for your life and well-being" does the child begin to change. More than once I've seen this play out in family therapy sessions. This illustrates the importance of being able to *describe* (remember the second What skill in Mindfulness**)** and express our emotions. Remember, one purpose of emotion is to motivate. When family members avoid talking about being scared for their child's welfare, typically the child becomes defensive and oppositional. When the family member says, "I'm scared," the child typically tunes in, reverses course, and responds favorably to what the parent is saying.

Your emotions are a tremendous resource. However, unless you can put the correct label on the emotion and communicate it, you are like a person who has money in their bank account and yet does not know how to write a check or use a debit card.

CHECK THE FACTS: EXAMPLE FROM THE BIG SCREEN

Caddyshack is a 1980 comedy that is considered a cult classic by many (Ramis & Kenney, 1980). The film stars Chevy Chase, Bill Murray, Rodney Dangerfield and Ted Knight, and is situated in a country club, around the game of golf. There are many amusing subplots such as the friction between carefree, fun-loving, and wealthy real estate developer Al Czervik (Dangerfield) and the uptight and pompous Judge Elihu Smails (Knight) who are both golf enthusiasts who belong to the club.

One of the funnier scenes happens at the club swimming pool. An elementary school-age boy is offered a candy bar by his mother. The lad, in an act of mischief, hurls the candy bar into the pool where no one notices it for several moments. Then…someone sees the candy bar floating on the surface, and this becomes (in DBT terms) a prompting event. What they see is a brown rectangular object, about 8 inches long, bobbing in the water. Someone yells "poopy!" another person shrieks, then everyone starts screaming in terror. They all flee the object, bounding out of the pool in a state of sheer panic. It is obvious the source of their terror was not the brown object, but their *interpretation* that this brown object was a bowel movement.

The next scene shows the pompous Judge Smails and his goody-goody wife supervising Carl (played by Bill Murray), who is the country club's handyman. The pool has been drained, and Carl is standing at the bottom of it in a full-body hazmat suit, complete with mask. He picks up the brown object with the pool strainer, removes his bio-mask, holds the object closer, studies it in detail, then sniffs it. The judge warns him to be careful. Carl says, "It's no worry!" then takes a bite out of the brown rectangular object. The judge's wife faints in horror.

This scene illustrates that it is not the prompting event alone that triggers our emotion (in this case, terror and disgust), but also our interpretation of the prompting event (the floating candy bar). This is why the Check the Facts skill is so important, and is the first skill to use when we experience extreme emotions. Sometimes our extreme emotions are prompted by misinterpretation, and when we discover our perception was incorrect, our emotions change quickly and for the better.

The Check the Facts skill is indispensable for emotion regulation.

INTERPRETATION—MISINTERPRETATION— "SOMETHIN' STUPID"

The song was number one on the charts for four weeks, and was burning up the radio in the summer of 1967. It was a father-daughter duet by Frank and Nancy Sinatra (Parks, 1967). The title was "Somethin' Stupid," referring to a person on a date believing they had said something klutzy in the conversation with the object of their infatuation.

This song is the backdrop for one of my most vivid memories from childhood. My uncle Johnny and aunt Marty were visiting us; my sister was six years old and was taking piano lessons. She played a song she learned for my aunt and uncle. Aunt Marty was known to be very straightforward and blunt, and perhaps this intimidated my sister a little bit. After my sister Jennifer was done playing the song, aunt Marty said, "Can you play 'Somethin' Stupid'?" My sister immediately burst into tears, ran to her bedroom and slammed the door shut.

DBT points out that that often it is not the prompting event, per se, that creates painful emotions or emotional dysregulation, rather it is our interpretation of the prompting event.

The story of "Somethin' Stupid" illustrates how our interpretation can be a misinterpretation. We fall into the trap of believing our interpretation is 100 percent reality, but DBT provides us with the Check the Facts skill to free us from the tyranny of believing that our first impression is always accurate.

As I think of it now, perhaps I should call my sister (now age 59) and explain the facts were different than her interpretation.

CHECK THE FACTS: PROMPTING EVENT—METAPHOR—DIRTY WINDSHIELD

Albert Ellis, one of the giants in the development of modern psychotherapy (especially cognitive behavioral therapies), reminded us that, as the ancient Greek philosophers pointed out, "It is not what happens, but our view of it" that determines our emotional response (Ellis, 1962). In DBT we call this our *interpretation* of the Prompting Event. An important place to start is realizing (mindfulness) that the prompting event and our interpretation of the event can be two very different things.

Just as some people look at the world through "rose-colored glasses" and see everything as wonderful (a very undialectical viewpoint), others look at the world through what I call "crap-colored glasses," seeing the world as completely filled with "bad," hostile, and negative realities. This is like having birds' crap all over the windshield of your car. As you drive your car, the world probably looks really "shitty" to you.

If you are in a DBT group, it is probable that you have had more than the average amount of shitty things happen to you. It is not your fault that your windshield was crapped upon, but it is your responsibility to now clean it off and begin to see the world more accurately. Dr Linehan points out this is what we are doing by using the Check the Facts skill, namely to separate our opinions and judgments from the facts themselves. Then, and only then, can we see the world as it really is.

CHECK THE FACTS: JUDGMENTS AND INTERPRETATIONS ABOUT OURSELVES—DON'T BELIEVE EVERYTHING YOU HEAR

Our minds are constantly turning out thoughts. It is important to realize that not all thoughts that pop up in our mind are accurate or true. In a similar therapy to DBT, Acceptance and Commitment Therapy or ACT (Hayes et al., 2012), we are taught that our thoughts and reality are two different things. Our thoughts may be an accurate perception of reality, but in many cases, they are not. If you struggle with depression, you likely experience multiple critical and judgmental thoughts pop up in your consciousness. These thoughts tell you that you are a bad person, you're not capable, you never do anything right, etc. If you're a person who struggles with anxiety, your mind may be manufacturing thoughts such as "something bad is about to happen" or "everyone thinks I'm stupid."

Often this propensity to respond to daily situations with a negative spin comes from our earlier learning experiences in childhood and/or adolescence. Some psychologists have referred to this phenomenon as "tapes" from our past. It is important to question what these "tapes" say.

When I graduated from high school, I secured a job working in the local factory making screwdrivers and drill bits. One of my parents responded with great anger (which I believe was really fear in disguise), telling me "You won't last in there half a day! That's a man's job!" Fortunately, I did not respond to this statement as if it were the "gospel truth" or absolute reality. I questioned it, hoping that I would actually succeed on the job. I spent the next two summers making lots of screwdrivers and drill bits, and was thus able to pay for college.

Marsha Linehan tells us how we can respond to these thoughts popping up in our head. In DBT, we take a mindful approach, simply *observing* the thoughts without endorsing them, embracing them, or fighting against them. They are just clouds in the sky, passing by. They come and they go. We observe them. No need to endorse them if they don't correspond with reality.

CHECK THE FACTS: PUT SERGEANT JOE FRIDAY ON THE CASE

Dragnet (Webb, 1951) was a TV show about two Los Angeles police detectives. Though the main characters were fictionalized, the story lines were adapted from real LAPD cases "with the names changed to protect the innocent." The lead detective was Sergeant Joe Friday, who was masterful at separating opinions, interpretations, and biases from the facts. His trademark statement was "just the facts." Friday would insert "just the facts" when he realized witnesses were starting to share opinions and interpretations (which are judgments). By keeping the facts separate from opinions, he prevented the investigation from jumping to erroneous conclusions that were based on interpretations. This resulted in Friday being extremely effective at getting to the truth.

My sons' school would rent out a small but charming amusement park one night a year, and students, parents, siblings, and teachers would enjoy a night of fun. By second grade, it was obvious that my younger son Nate was much taller than his classmates—his pediatrician estimates he will eventually be six feet, nine inches tall. One of his classmates was a little person, much shorter than her classmates. Nate and I ran across her at the amusement park, but I was surprised that he did not say "hi" to her. My worry was he thought himself too cool to talk to this small person. But I checked the facts, later asking him why he had pretended not to notice her. "I was afraid she would make fun of me for being so tall." This illustrates how our interpretation of the motives of others can be tremendously inaccurate. (It also illustrates how Nate's fear was probably not accurate, created by unneeded worry and separating him from others).

The older I get (and the longer I teach DBT skills), the more I realize how many people believe their opinions, interpretations, "jumped to" conclusions, and judgments are facts. The more we can separate our interpretations from the facts, and just stick to the facts, the more our life can liberated from emotional suffering stemming from misperception.

Want to reduce painful emotions and unneeded suffering? Put Joe Friday on the case. Check the Facts.

ACTION URGE—WHEN TO CHOOSE TO USE THE OPPOSITE ACTION SKILL

Recently I had a doctor's appointment and they asked for my insurance card. I did not have it. As a result, my appointment was delayed as they attempted to access my insurance coverage by other means. After 40 minutes, it appeared they would not be able to allow me to see the doctor. I was pacing around in this huge waiting room, becoming increasingly frustrated. On an end table was a small stand holding a stack of brochures about some medical procedure. I was so frustrated in that moment that I had the sudden urge to kick the stand and the brochures the way a football player would try to kick a field goal. I could just imagine the brochures flying all over the waiting room.

What I experienced was an *action urge*. We have action urges for every emotion. When we experience the urges, we must ask ourselves whether to use Problem Solving or Opposite Action to deal the urge. It is crucial to choose the right skill for the situation. The key question is, "Would kicking the brochures all over the waiting room be an effective way to deal with my frustration?"

What would have happened if I had made the kick? The first thing that would have happened would be security would have been called, and they would have handed me over to the police. I might have spent a night in jail and I certainly would not be welcome back at that medical office. Would that have increased or decreased my sense of frustration? Thankfully I used Opposite Action, and by choosing to be gentle, kind, and even apologetic to the office staff for my agitation, I actually calmed down rather than continuing to rev up. It is a common myth that we must act on our extreme emotions to let the pressure off, but the persons who endorse this viewpoint are usually the most volatile. Opposite action is the way to cool down. Plus, Opposite Action spared me the indignity of being handcuffed.

It is always important to take the time to ask yourself, "Is this an effective way to deal with my emotion?" if not use **Opposite Action.**

ACTION URGE—A LESSON FROM JAWS

Sometimes we struggle to use our skills because we don't recognize how quickly an emotion is coming upon us. A prompting event happens, and before we realize it we are engaging in a self-defeating behavior such as fighting, using substances, harming our self, etc. Sometimes our emotions sneak up on us, and prompt us to act before we can think.

Mindfulness is the key to not letting an emotion and its companion action urge to sneak up on us in this manner. If we are aware of the emotion beginning to bubble up, then we can use our skills before automatically acting on the Action Urge. We need to be like a meteorologist, seeing the conditions for a storm *before* the storm hits.

The movie *Jaws* (Spielberg et al., 1975) is about a gigantic shark that terrorizes a small New England town. The shark kills several swimmers, the town is terrorized, and the economy of the small town is in jeopardy because it is centered around tourism at the beach.

One of the key aspects of the film that made it such a monumental hit was the music composed by John Williams (the same composer who wrote the music for *Star Wars*). Viewers did not see the shark coming, it was below the surface, but they knew when it was getting closer by Williams ominous and iconic music. "Da-dum," you knew the shark was somewhere in the vicinity. A second "da-dum," you knew the shark was getting closer. When the stream of "da-dums" was continuous you knew the shark was about to strike, pulling the person under to their death.

Our task is to be more attune to our emotions, aware when the initial "da-dums" start, and prepare to use the appropriate skill. We can't wait until the emotion is at full volume and the Action Urge has us in its teeth. Listen for the first tremors of the problem emotion, the "da-dums" of an unregulated emotional firestorm before it happens. Listen for the ominous music. Then use your skills to get out of the water!

SUDS SCALE: ABOVE 70—WISE MIND IS NOT GETTING ENOUGH OXYGEN

The movie *The Right Stuff* (Brubaker & Kaufman, 1983) is about America's test pilots in the 1940s through the 1960s, as well as our first astronauts in the Mercury space program. One of the characters of this true-life film is Colonel Chuck Yeager, one of the greatest test pilots of that era. The film portrays him as being frustrated because the astronauts are getting great media coverage while he has not (yet) been given permission to fly the Air Force's most recent jet. Without clearance from his superiors, Yeager got into the plane, took off, and flew it as fast and as high as it would go. He ran into a problem when he got to a record high altitude: the air was so thin that the jet's engine was not taking in enough oxygen to continue to burn. The engine cut out and all of a sudden Yeager's plane was falling from the sky. Fortunately, Yeager was able to eject before the plane crashed and burst into flames.

When our Subjective Units of Distress Scale goes above 70, we are flying at a very high altitude, one in which Wise Mind becomes more compromised the higher up the scale we go. When we go above 70, Emotion Mind dominates, and does not let Reasonable Mind to have enough oxygen to function. For this reason, before we use any other skills, we need to use skills to bring our degree of emotional intensity back down under 70, where Wise Mind functions well. We do not want our Wise Mind engine to cut out on us, resulting in bad decisions and regrettable, self-defeating behavior.

SUDS SCALE ELEVATED LEADS TO UNFORTUNATE ACTING ON ACTION URGE

All of us have urges to do all sorts of things: if we are in Wise Mind, we look at the urge, think about the likely result that would occur if we act on the urge, and refrain from the urge if it would lead to undesirable consequences. When our SUDS is above 70 (and especially when we are in the 90s), we are less apt to make Wise-Minded choices. I want to emphasize that even if we are intelligent, accomplished, and successful, we can impulsively react to our Action Urges, leading to a self-defeating outcome.

This is a story of a person who was very accomplished, disciplined, intelligent, and successful. He was the football coach at a major university, and the players he coached over a three decade span felt very indebted to him for his guidance and support, not so much in football, but in becoming good and successful human beings who would "pay it forward," making the world a better place. Nonetheless when his SUDS went sky-high, he acted on his urge without thinking.

Woody Hayes was the head football coach at The Ohio State University from 1951–1978. Coach Hayes lead his teams to five National Championships (1954, 1957, 1961, 1968, 1970) as well as 13 Big Ten Conference championships. Can you imagine the intelligence and discipline it would take to accomplish these feats?

However, there were times Hayes did not effectively regulate his emotions, especially anger. Throughout his career, when angry, he threw punches and charged at photographers, camera men, and referees. In the 1978 Gator Bowl, Hayes let his emotions get the best of him again. With two minutes left in the game and Ohio State driving towards a potential game-winning field goal, Clemson nose guard Charlie Bauman intercepted an Ohio State pass, and went out of bounds near the Ohio State sidelines, Hayes ran up to Bauman and punched him in the throat. In the subsequent brawl between the two teams, one of Ohio State's offensive linemen tried to intervene and cool down the volatile coach, but then Hayes turned on his own player and had to be restrained by the OSU defensive coordinator. The next day Coach Hayes was subsequently dismissed from his three decade reign of the Buckeyes, and his coaching career was over.

For me, the moral of this story is that no matter how bright, accomplished, and hardworking we may be, this does not eradicate the need to stay mindful of how high our emotions are on the SUDS scale, nor the need to deliberately stop and think about whether our Action Urge in the moment is a good or bad idea. When totally in Emotion Mind, the Action Urge seems like the right thing to do, but the consequences tell us otherwise. In his own description of what happened at that fateful Gator Bowl game, Hayes said, "'I didn't hit [Bauman] to hurt him.' Hayes said later, "It only hurt me. You can't always explain everything" (Lombardo, 2005, 238). What the iconic coach was saying was that his punch to Bauman made absolutely no logical (Reasonable Mind) sense. Acting on pure Emotion Mind only hurt him.

Coach Ara Parseghian, who was at one time an assistant to Woody, described this Emotion Mind phenomenon: "Woody as the most emotional guy I'd ever seen [on the field]. But off the field he was like a father [to his players]. He was really like two different people" (Lombardo, 2005, in the foreword).

When I have been over 70 on the SUDS scale, I have done things I greatly regretted. My patients have likewise thrown and broke cell phones, wrecked automobiles, punched holes in walls, broken windows, tried to fight police officers, and called their mothers the most insulting and derogatory names imaginable. The truth is, we all have something in common with Coach Hayes. When we lose our cool, acting on urges becomes a totally emotional enterprise.

On the DBT Emotion Regulation Handout 5 (Linehan, 2015a, p. 213), "Model of Describing Emotions", I emphasize the space between Action urges and Actions (both at the bottom of the large rectangle). Between the urge and the action, we have to be mindful enough to know where our emotions are, cool them down if over 70, and make sure we are in Wise Mind before executing any action.

ACTION URGE: SUBJECTIVE UNITS OF DISTRESS SCALE (SUDS)—GETTING YOUR SUDS BELOW 70

A number of years ago, I experienced a very stressful situation. During a routine checkup with my physician, I found out I had an elevated PSA score which can, among other things, be an early warning sign of prostate cancer. I knew that other factors can cause elevated PSA, but I still was extremely worried and anxious, knowing I *might* have prostate cancer. My SUDS score was well above 70.

I play guitar in a rock and roll band and, during this time, we had a show. We kicked off with a song by Creedence Clearwater Revival, but from the beginning of the song I realized something was terribly wrong with the sound of my guitar. I tried to figure out why the song sounded so bad, and thought perhaps one of my strings was way out of tune. By the very end of the song it dawned on me why the song sounded so bad; I was playing the wrong Creedence Clearwater Revival song and it was in a different key!

As it turned out, I did not have prostate cancer. But my elevated anxiety led me to do something that I would never fall prey to under 70. Whenever our SUDS level gets over 70, priority one is to get it back down.

CHECK THE FACTS SKILL: "I FEEL LIKE A FAILURE"

There are times in most people's lives when they may feel like a failure. A compelling story and movie illustrates this is *It's a Wonderful Life* (Capra, 1946). George Bailey, played by Jimmy Stewart, is a struggling banker who, on Christmas Eve, feels like a failure. George is drunk and standing on a bridge, thinking about committing suicide. George's guardian angel is sent to save him from his suicidal urges. The angel realizes that George's view of his life is overlooking many of the objective facts of his life. George is only looking at his stressors, which come from running a struggling Savings and Loan in a small town. The situation is made worse when his uncle loses $8,000 from the Savings and Loan.

The guardian angel, Clarence, intervenes by reminding George of all the good he has done in his life by showing him an alternative timeline in which his contributions never happened. This film is a favorite at the holidays, and I don't want to ruin or spoil it for you by giving away all the details. However it is important to note that when the angel points out the many positive contributions and how people's lives would be much worse without George, he is *willing* to accept this information into his view of himself, his life, and his importance to people in the town. In DBT terminology, he is willing to Turn his Mind back towards reality (you will learn about this in the Distress Tolerance module).

Are you *willing* to turn your mind back in the direction of reality when your therapist, friends, colleagues, etc. point out how your life is not a failure? Are you willing to look at the importance of the contributions you have made? It is a choice: are we willing to **Check the Facts**? Are you willing to **Turn Your Mind** in the direction of treating yourself fairly when looking at your life?

CHECK THE FACTS: INTERPRETATION CAN BE WILDLY WRONG

My eldest son Noah was nine years old when we went to the theater to see *The Lego Movie* (Abbate et al., 2014). As we left the theater, he said to me "Dad, don't you think Mom is like Lord Business (the villain)?" I thought my son was saying his mother was controlling, bossy, and self-centered (like Lord Business). I was shocked that he would say such a thing about his mama, but I decided to explore his thinking rather than jump to conclusions, to stick with "just the facts" of what Noah said. The fact was his verbatim statement was "Don't you think Mom is like Lord Business?" I asked Noah, "So how is Mom like Lord Business?" He responded, "She has really long legs, just like him."

Many times, we confuse our interpretation for the facts. The fact was Noah said, "Mom is like Lord Business." My interpretation was wildly wrong. Often there is a world of difference between the facts and our interpretation of what they mean. Can you see how straying from the facts into interpretations and judgments ("he is disrespecting his mother!") can lead to many painful emotions and interpersonal conflict?

Here is another example of how our interpretation can be wildly wrong. One of my therapy patients was an 18-year-old woman who just graduated from high school and was headed to her freshman year of college. She was going out of state and knew nobody else headed to this school, and as such was assigned a potluck roommate, someone she had never met. . Mid-summer, my client emailed the new roommate, but received no reply. After several weeks, my client sent another email, but again there was no reply. She began worry. What was going on with this roommate? Was she conceited? Just aloof? Was this going to be a really weird roommate with no personal skills? My client was extremely anxious, feeling tormented about sharing intimate space with this person for an entire academic year. How dreadful could this make her freshman year? The week before she left for college another piece of information emerged. She finally got an email from her future roommate, who shared that she just returned from a six-week wilderness canoe trip, where she had no access to the internet. The roommate was excited to meet my client.

The fact was that my client e-mailed her roommate, and the e-mail was not answered for six weeks. Sticking to just the facts, just what we know, can save us from a mountain of unnecessary worry.

OPPOSITE ACTION—ANGER—WHAT THE RESEARCH SAYS

When I was a psychologist in training in the 1980s, I witnessed at several practicum sites therapists who would encourage clients to deal with their anger by pounding a bat or racquetball racquet on a padded chair. The idea was that the person had a lot of anger inside him or her, and that once they "got it out" they would feel better because the anger would be "out" of them. These therapists would encourage clients to get themselves as angry as possible and beat the hell out of the chair or pillow. One company even manufactured specialty "therapy bats" specifically for this use. I never saw this help anyone, and I was perplexed as how this would help people get to a better place.

What the scientific research has subsequently told us is that this kind of acting out of rage actually worsens peoples' anger, and they leave the experience more agitated. (For a detailed explanation of this see the book *Anger: The Misunderstood Emotion* [Travis, 1989]).

When the degree of anger you are experiencing does not fit the facts of the situation, the solution is Opposite Action. In this situation, revving up or indulging your anger to go above 70 on the SUDS (Subjective Units of Distress Scale) is only throwing gasoline on the fire of your emotional problem. If you get burned time after time when getting angry, it may be the time to switch to Opposite Action.

OPPOSITE ACTION: ALL THE WAY—BECOMING A CHARACTER ACTOR

Marsha Linehan tells us when using the Opposite Action skill to do the opposite action "all the way" (Linehan, 2015a, p. 231) It is important not do Opposite Action in a half-hearted way, but rather to fully do the action while also practicing the right attitude and emotions.

I often suggest to DBT students to practice Opposite Action and pretend that they are a character actor. When Tom Hanks played Forrest Gump (Finerman et al., 1994), he became Forrest Gump. He saw the world as a person with an IQ of 75 who grew up in Alabama with a single parent. He became Forrest Gump, including the innocent nature and sense of goodwill towards others.

To practice Opposite Action, we have to throw ourselves into what we are doing, even when it feels unnatural. It may take the resolve of a character actor to be kind and gentle when we are not feeling it, or confident and bold when we are fearful. Remember, doing the Opposite Action is not just about the action, but the mindset, the emotions, and the perception. There is no "just going through the motions." We have to *be* and *feel* the action, as well as doing it!

USING OPPOSITE ACTION TO CONQUER SHAME: MY OWN EXAMPLE—SINGING IN PUBLIC

Opposite Action is used to change our emotional response to situations when our emotional response does not fit the facts of the situation, or when our emotional reaction is not effective.

Yes, it is possible to change our emotions when we use this powerful DBT skill.

Growing up I was taught to be ashamed of my voice, especially my singing voice. When one is ashamed of one's voice, one is ashamed of one of the most intimate parts of oneself. This was problematic for me because I did play guitar and wanted to be in a rock band, as well as do folk music on acoustic guitar. Finally, after getting out of graduate school in my late thirties, I took the plunge and played at a coffee house, just me, my voice, and my acoustic guitar. Looking back, I realize that it didn't sound that good. The problem with my voice wasn't with my God-given abilities, but rather that I felt so ashamed of putting myself out there. My bodily reaction to the emotion of shame led to me tightening the muscles in my throat, which in turn altered the sound of my voice in a negative direction. Also this caused me to not fully project my singing voice. Rather, I kind of sheepishly held back and muffled what I was doing; the result did not sound very good, which in turn reinforced my sense of shame about putting myself forth in public and wanting others to listen to me sing.

However, after this fitful start, I began to just throw myself out there, not caring what other people thought about me. As such, I began to sing with confidence, feeling the emotions that the words conveyed. I didn't realize it at the time, but I was practicing Opposite Action. The result was my voice sounded good enough. To be sure, I am not a great vocalist like Whitney Houston, Harry Connick Jr., or Adele. If I rated my voice on a one-to-ten scale (with one being a person who is completely tone deaf) I would say it's about a six, maybe a 6.5 on an exceptional day. I tell people "I can carry a tune in a bucket."

What is true is there was no reason for me to feel grossly ashamed of my singing voice. Reacting to the sound of my voice as if it were "terrible" did not fit the facts of the situation, nor was it effective in accomplishing my musical and leisure goals. Most importantly, I used Opposite Action to change my emotional reaction to my voice.

EXAMPLES OF WHEN TO USE OPPOSITE ACTION

- Feeling insecure at a social gathering, with an Action Urge to withdraw or "blend into the background?" It is time to use Opposite Action and connect with others.

- Feeling ashamed due to being unemployed, with an Action Urge to conceal this from others. It is time to use Opposite Action by openly telling others of your unemployment, your frustration at this, and your desire to find a job. (Perhaps by telling your friends, they will give you some useful leads to follow!)
- Feeling angry about a loved one's behavior, yet feeling very anxious when thinking about talking directly about this, with the Action Urge to deal with this anxiety and the urge to conceal your feelings about the issue? Use Opposite Action to do the opposite of avoiding—address the problem!

WHY OPPOSITE ACTION? METAPHOR: BENADRYL FOR ALLERGIES

Why do we take Benadryl for allergic reactions? During an allergic reaction, our immune system overreacts to non-threatening stimuli as if the substance were a dangerous attacker. The immune system's counterattack (based on its faulty perception), is what causes our symptoms as it attacks our own cells (as well as the foreign substance). When taken, Benadryl causes our immune system to behave in exactly the opposite fashion, allowing the substance to enter the body, rather than attacking the substance, with our own cells becoming "collateral damage."

With Opposite Action, we are training our psychological system, our mind, to react differently to people and situations. Opposite Action is, in a sense, psychological Benadryl. Think of the value of being able to react with calmness rather than out-of-control rage to a person that might be criticizing or invalidating you. You can then respond to this person in Wise Mind, speaking up in an effective manner, telling them how you want to be treated. By responding in a less intense fashion, you are also, in effect, telling yourself that the critical remark is not really worthy of a dramatic response ("sticks and stones may break my bones, but your words will not harm me").

Sometimes, we can forget what the letters DBT stand for. The "BT" is shorthand for "Behavior Therapy." One of the cardinal principles of Behavior Therapy, proven through both scientific research and clinical experience, is that one of the most effective ways to change our emotions is by changing our behavior.

Why change our behavior to change our emotional response? Simply put, because it works!

COMBINING OPPOSITE ACTION AND PROBLEM SOLVING

There are times we need to use both Opposite Action and Problem Solving to deal with difficult emotions and the accompanying urges that can potentially get us in trouble. First, we must use Opposite Action in response to the immediate urge. For example, if you were anxious and your action urge was to go to a bar and get drunk, Opposite Action would be to go away from the bar because getting drunk is not an effective way to deal with your emotion. Next, you could engage in Problem Solving to change the circumstances that are making you anxious.

Members of my DBT group felt overwhelmed by the idea of putting these two skills together, starting with one, then combining it with the other. I was trying to think of a simple example of how we can combine Opposite Action and Problem Solving, then I realized there's one that we do every day. When we have the urge to urinate or defecate, we use Opposite Action—we hold it in. But then we must engage in Problem Solving to deal with the urge, namely we need to locate a restroom, pursue the quickest route to get there, and dispose of our waste.

Did you realize that you were already using Opposite Action and Problem Solving in your everyday life?

ABC PLEASE: ACCUMULATE POSITIVE EMOTIONAL EXPERIENCES: METAPHOR—THE POSITIVE EMOTIONS BANK

Imagine that today is the last day of the month; you need to write a check to make your rent or house payment. Until now, you really haven't given this much thought, you have not been working, have not been making or saving money, because the rent was not due until today. Few of us would get ourselves into this sort of jam. We realize (unless we have a mega-trust fund) that we need to be diligently making and saving money for our bills *before* they arrive.

Sadly, we may not have applied this same strategy to our psychological life. As such, we may find ourselves being "emotionally overdrawn" much of the time. Overwhelming, painful, stressful emotions may greatly outnumber the positive experiences and emotions.

DBT gives us permission and encourages us to *proactively accumulate* positive emotional experiences every day. Passively wishing that today will be good is not the DBT way.

My wife once read a book titled *Rich Dad, Poor Dad* (Kiyosaki & Lechter, 1998) that documented that (sadly) persons growing up in a financially poor family are often not taught about accumulating, saving, and investing money. As such, they are unlikely to know how to improve their financial lives (or even realize they can improve their financial lives), and they often remain poor, even when they are hard working. DBT teaches us to be mindful of our behavior and choices, and to accumulate emotional wealth.

When I teach this component to my DBT skills groups, I draw a bank on the dry-erase board (a stick figure house with a big dollar sign mounted on the roof). Every day is an opportunity to make deposits in our Positive Emotions Bank account (see the Pleasant Events Diary in your DBT Workbook; Linehan, 2015, p. 295).

ABC—ACCUMULATE POSITIVE EMOTIONS—
POSITIVE FEELINGS FACTORY

When I teach the ABC PLEASE skills, I often draw a factory on the easel board, and ask the group what is being manufactured in this factory (of course they have no idea). I describe this at the "Positive Feelings/Emotions Factory."

One of your tasks in this module is to invest yourself in the manufacturing business. Just like computers, automobiles, or musical instruments do not just appear out of thin air, positive emotional experiences will not just produce themselves; most of these experiences will start with you doing something that will create happiness, joy, peace, love, enjoyment, or meaning.

The place to begin your start-up in this manufacturing enterprise is the "Pleasant Events Diary" as well as the Values and Priorities Checklist in your DBT workbook (Linehan, 2015a, p. 295).

ACCUMULATING POSITIVE EMOTIONS—MAKE SURE YOUR BICYCLE HAS BOTH WHEELS

The Accumulate Positive Emotions skill is comprised of two components: accumulating positive emotions in the short term by engaging in pleasant events (fun stuff, see the Pleasant Events List on pp. 249–251 of the DBT Skills Training Handouts and Worksheets, Linehan, 2015a) and in the long term living according to one's Values and Priorities (pp. 252–255).

I often draw a bicycle on the dry erase board to illustrate the importance of both. If you have a bicycle, and one wheel is stolen, the bike will go nowhere. I say this, in part, because there was a time in my life where I lived a life of great self-sacrifice, devoting myself almost exclusively to a noble cause (a value), believing I would be greatly rewarded in the long run with happiness. It did not work. Pleasure is a part of life. Going without it is like trying to go without water. Some people live by a similar myth, thinking if they live a semi-martyr-like existence, denying themselves of pleasure, fun, recreation, hobbies, etc., the universe or God will reward them with happiness. If it turns out this way, that's great. But if you have been taught this or believe it yourself, you no doubt would not be in DBT right now. Cyndi Lauper sang that girls just want to have fun but she could have also sang girls just *need* to have fun. Boys too.

On the other hand, many people try to ride a happiness bicycle with only the pleasure wheel, and are missing the living by priorities and values wheel. See the next several metaphors below to understand that fun stuff alone cannot create enough happiness to keep you afloat.

ACCUMULATING POSITIVE EMOTIONS BY PRACTICING YOUR VALUES—TALE OF A MISFIT ELF

When it comes to *Accumulating* positive emotions (ABC PLEASE), it is important that you live by *your* values, otherwise you will accumulate very little positive emotion. If try to live by someone else's values, you may be invalidating yourself.

The original Rudolph the Red-Nosed Reindeer TV Christmas special (1964) was far ahead of its time and illustrated this truth. Hermie was an unhappy elf, laboring in Santa's workshop. The problem was that he didn't like making toys. When other elves heard of this, they were astonished, and some were offended. In his heart of hearts, Hermie knew he wanted to be a dentist. No one validated Hermie's value or goal. And eventually he and the other "misfit," Rudolph, leave Christmas Town due to a lack of validation by the rest of the town. As the story progresses, Hermie eventually saves the day, using his budding dentistry skills to pull the teeth of the dreaded Abominable Snowman, thus taking away the dreaded beast's power to terrorize Christmas Town.

This child's story reflects important truths for persons of every age—specifically that it is important to stay true to our values and priorities. Even when our efforts do not meet with immediate validation, it is important that *we* validate them (assuming they are Wise-Minded values). The pursuit and practice of our values and priorities will culminate in useful contributions to society *and* they will create for us the positive emotions we need.

Authors note: I was six years old when Rudolph the Red-Nosed Reindeer Christmas special first aired on TV, and I was absolutely terrified of the Abominable Snowman.

ABC PLEASE: ACCUMULATE POSITIVE EMOTIONS IN THE SHORT TERM AND LONG TERM: VALUES AND PRIORITIES—TEACHING POINT-CREATING POSITIVE EMOTIONS THROUGH VALUE-BASED LIVING

It is important to note that it is unwise to try to create positive emotional experiences *solely* by the pursuit of pleasure. Pleasure is a good thing, and DBT encourages us to seek it out (see the Pleasant Events List) in Linehan, 2015a, p. 249). However, our approach must be dialectically complemented by values-based living to successfully create significant positive emotion.

There is an episode of the old TV series *The Twilight Zone* (Beaumont & Brahm, 1960) in which a man named Rocky Valentine loves to gamble dies and wakes up in the afterlife. (This episode is in season one, episode 28, entitled "A Nice Place to Visit.") He is greeted by a man named Pip, who grants him his every wish. Rocky reasons that Pip is his guardian angel. Pip supplies Rocky with an endless stream of cash and access to a casino, where, to his further amazement, he wins every time he gambles. He also is given an unlimited supply of alcohol and beautiful women to consort with who never turn down his advances. Rocky is experiencing delight for the first several weeks of this new existence. However, after a month he becomes bored; this existence is too predictable. After several months his boredom is excruciating. Then Rocky says to Pip, if he had known that heaven was so boring, he would never have chosen to go there. Pip replied, "What gives you the idea that you are in heaven?"

Substantial happiness is not built on pleasure alone, but requires values-based living. I share this example with my DBT groups to distinguish between pleasure and happiness that results from values-based living; if I ride a roller coaster I will enjoy myself for the three to four minutes I am on the coaster, but then my positive feeling drifts away. However, if I take my two teenage sons on the roller coaster, the happiness that stems from my memory of this experience may last the rest of my life, because I am fulfilling my value of being a supportive and devoted father.

Both pleasure- and values-based living are important for happiness. One without the other is like a bicycle that is missing s wheel.

BUILD MASTERY—YOU CAN BE A MASTER!

Marsha Linehan defines mastery as "doing things that make you feel competent, self-confident, in control, and capable of mastering things" (Linehan, 2015b, p. 392). Notice she does not include "perfect" or "better than anyone else" in the definition. I once had a very intelligent and successful client who, every time he took on a task, would say, "My goal is to do it better than anyone else ever has done or could do." "Why is that important to do?" I asked. We explored how this man felt he needed to have a stream of super-human accomplishments to even feel okay about himself. No wonder he frequently felt overwhelmed and depressed. No wonder it was a struggle to abstain from getting high every day of the week.

If you have equated mastery with doing things perfectly, disconnect those two things—they are not the same thing. Look at what Dr Linehan says about mastery: "the idea is to generate a sense of accomplishment" (p. 392). Perfectionism always leads to feeling imperfect and like a failure. Perfectionism is the enemy of accomplishment, but few people realize this.

Dr Linehan tells us to "plan for success, not failure" by realizing there are three categories of endeavor:

1. Easy
2. Difficult but possible
3. Impossible

Dr Linehan tells us to pick the middle path between too easy and too hard, finding something that pushes us to improve our skills, but that will not result in a "crash and burn." As we encounter success, we then need to gradually increase the difficulty of our endeavor over time. The goal is not to avoid imperfection, but to increase accomplishment. If you have perfectionistic tendencies, you probably think that accomplishment is impossible apart from perfectionism. But usually, perfectionism is a huge roadblock to accomplishment. If this is you, I recommend the book *Never Good Enough* by Monica Ramirez Basco (1999). This book has helped a number of my clients escape the cage of perfectionism and live effectively.

If I start playing a new and somewhat difficult song on the guitar, my goal is to be able to play it somewhat correctly, which is better than not being able to play it at all. As I achieve this, I then work to play it more correctly, eliminating mistakes, playing it closer to the original. If perfect was my goal, I would collapse into despair.

I recently saw a poster with a saying by Dr Wayne Dyer that read, "My goal is not to be better than anyone else, but to be better that I used to be" (I have no other citation other than I saw this on a poster where I work). If you only post one inspirational statement on your refrigerator in your lifetime, this would not be a bad choice.

Needlepoint, gardening, karate, pottery, crossword puzzles, restoring antique automobiles, playing an instrument: they are all good avenues to build mastery, to feel accomplished.

EMOTION REGULATION: VALUES AND PRIORITIES

Have you ever seen the aftermath of a building that has been demolished? What is left in its place is a vacant lot. If the lot is left vacant, it does not stay vacant for long. Where once there was just a dirt lot, soon there will be a garden of weeds blighting the landscape. This points to the importance of not leaving a lot vacant. One must plant grass, trees or flowers; if the space is not filled up, it is an invitation for an influx of weeds.

If you are studying DBT, it is because your life is full of difficult, painful, and unpleasant emotions, and you have no doubt spent a lot of effort pulling these "weeds," only to have more grow back. This has happened, in large part due to the fact that no one taught you how to plant the grass, trees, and flowers that could secure your emotional life. The Values and Priorities List (Linehan, 2015a, pp. 253–255) is the nursery where you can get many of the plants to build your life worth living.

COPE AHEAD OF TIME WITH DIFFICULT EMOTIONAL SITUATIONS—DEER CAUGHT IN THE HEADLIGHTS AND FIRE DRILL METAPHORS

"He froze like a deer caught in the headlights." Many of us (myself included) can personally identify with this metaphor, having been the deer caught in the headlights at some point in our lives. When overwhelmed, we become behaviorally frozen. However, inaction is only one of the problems that arises when we are overwhelmed by an emotion. Many of us become frozen into old, very predictable yet ineffective or downright self-defeating patterns of behavior that create more misery. Our stereotyped response style may be a pattern of self-harm, drug or alcohol abuse, physical or verbal aggression when we get angry, withdrawing when depressed...and the list goes on.

Behavior therapy (and DBT is a behavior therapy) indicates we need to have a **behavior action plan** for just such occasions (Mueser, et al., 2003). A great example of this is the fire drill. Schools conduct fire drills to teach students and staff the specific sequence of behaviors to engage in should a fire occur. Drills are practiced over and over to assure that the response to the alarm becomes second nature. All practicing starts *before* an actual fire ever happens. Practicing the drill repeatedly helps the students to not panic and helps them avoid behavior that would actually increase danger (fighting over who gets out the door first, pushing, running, and creating panic—a situation where some could be trampled.)

When putting together a behavior action plan, talk with your therapist about using the Opposite Action skill (Linehan, 2015a, p. 231). In the past, your Action Urge (to attack when someone hurts your feelings, harm yourself when anxious, abuse substances when lonely) has not been successful in helping you regulate your emotion, nor has your action achieved what you would define as a successful outcome.

DBT emphasizes what works. If a behavior does not help you, be prepared to trade it in for a *more effective* behavior.

A last statement about Coping Ahead of Time. It is important to anticipate what situations may happen *before* they occur, and train yourself to go into your behavior action plan immediately! Schools never wait until they have an actual fire to practice the drill!

COPE AHEAD OF TIME WITH DIFFICULT AND UNPLEASANT EMOTIONAL SITUATIONS: THE THREE LITTLE PIGS

The story of the Three Little Pigs is a great metaphor for Coping Ahead of Time with difficult emotional situations. The three little pigs set out to build houses. The first pig wanted to minimize his effort and maximize his play time, so he chose to build his house of straw. The second pig was not quite as irresponsible, but he does to build his house of sticks, which allowed him to go outside and play much sooner as well. The third pig took his time and built his house out of bricks, and thus did not get to play as much.

Think of the painful, difficult, and unwanted emotions that overwhelm you, turning your life into chaos: these emotions are the Big Bad Wolf. It is not a question of if the Big Bad Wolf is going to come your way, but *when* he is going to come your way. Your objective is to build the house that can withstand the Big Bad Wolf, who huffs and puffs and tries to blow your house down. Coping Ahead of Time takes just that—you have to anticipate when you are most at risk to have extreme emotions, and then build a structure of coping skills that will shield you from these emotions. You must start building the house *before* the Big Bad Wolf shows up.

When I meet with people prior to them joining one of my DBT groups, I point out that they are committing to sacrificing their time and some money to begin a building project. Sacrifice is involved, one must give up some play time. Also it will take some time for the entire structure to be in place. This will not be quick and easy. As such, I frequently tell people, "If your life does not suck, you may not want to join this group," because it involves an investment of time, effort, and money. However, if the Big Bad Wolf has huffed and puffed and blown a person's house down, this investment in studying and learning DBT is a real value.

COPE AHEAD OF TIME WITH EMOTIONALLY DIFFICULT SITUATIONS—HARRY MOORE'S DICTUM

For several years, I successfully participated in Weight Watchers, losing significant weight and keeping it off. Our leader, Harry Moore, had a number of valuable pointers that were examples of what Marsha Linehan and DBT would term the Cope Ahead of Time skill. Most of us in Weight Watchers were emotional overeaters—that is, we would eat as a form of coping with our emotions when we were bored, anxious, depressed, lonely, etc.

Harry would help us *Cope Ahead of Time* with these emotions and situations. One of the things Harry said he does when going to a party (where there would be bountiful delicious food) was make himself the promise "to leave when the food begins looking more interesting than the people." If emotions are prompting us to act on one of our Problem Behaviors, leaving before acting on the action urge may be the best option. (In this case, notice that leaving the party at this points is also the Opposite Action skill: we move away from rather than towards the food.)

Harry also told us to not go to such a party when hungry, making sure we have had adequate protein ahead of time, which combats the physical sense of hunger. Again, the idea was to Cope Ahead of Time, not wait until we are hungry and faced with limitless and appealing fatty and sugary foods.

Today I am 60 pounds lighter. Thanks, Harry, for helping me Cope Ahead of Time!

PLEASE: TREAT PHYSICAL ILLNESS

I once did counseling with a young woman who was a healthcare professional. Over our many sessions, I had heard many stories about her father whom she described as a loving, supportive, and kind man who was financially very successful, yet always there for his daughter when she needed his support. She began to worry when her father began experiencing physical pain, but refused the family's pleas to go to the doctor and have this checked out. After about a year of avoiding the doctor, he finally went because the pain just kept getting worse and worse. The news was bad—he had stage four cancer and would only live a few more months. After he died, my patient told me about an unfortunate truth; when her father finally went to the doctor at age 64, it was the first time he had seen a doctor since age 18, when he was required to have a complete physical to enlist in the US Navy.

Many people avoid doctors, dentists, and health care professionals for a variety of reasons, with perhaps fear being the most likely motivation to avoid them. The second may be the general discomfort of a relative stranger examining our body. But whatever the cause, avoiding the doctor is, in such cases, a decision to be un-mindful, to avoid knowing what is going on in our bodies.

With the PLEASE skills (Linehan, 2015a, p. 294), we take care of our mind by taking care of our body. It is very difficult to feel emotionally good when our body is hurting and suffering. Many of our hurts and maladies are easily treated—what holds us back from getting them fixed?

DBT is built on the foundation of mindfulness. Choosing to avoid the doctor is choosing to be *unmindful*.

PLEASE: AVOID MOOD ALTERING SUBSTANCES— PENNY WISE, POUND FOOLISH

"Penny wise, pound foolish" is an expression that many younger readers may not be familiar with. The term "pound" refers to the English unit of currency that is sort of the equivalent of the US dollar (actually one British pound at the time of this writing is equivalent to one dollar, 26 cents in US currency). Penny wise, pound foolish refers to a behavior that results in a small financial gain in the short run, but a huge loss in the long run.

Let me give an example of my own penny-wise-pound-foolishness. Once upon time, I had an older automobile that had part of the exhaust system rust through, causing a lot of noise and exhaust to escape. As I looked at this part in the garage, I decided that all I needed to replace were the parts of the system that looked to be very rusty, and I retained several parts, thus saving several hundred dollars—penny wise. Several months later another part of the exhaust system succumbed to rust, but this time it caused the whole exhaust system to fall off in traffic. I lost the whole exhaust system, costing well over a thousand dollars—pound foolish.

The PLEASE skill: Avoid mood-altering drugs (Linehan, 2015a, p. 294) is a way to avoid the penny wise/pound foolish mistake. Why do people take drugs? The short answer is drugs make individuals feel better, but this is the penny wise trap. For example, alcohol calms us down, relaxes us, and makes us less self-conscious. The problem is, this effect lasts only for a few hours, and if a person drinks excessively they experience what is known as "the rebound effect," where not only does the relaxation wear off, but the drinker then becomes tenser and more nervous. This unpleasant state will last far longer than the brief period of relaxation. When a person is physically addicted to alcohol, the rebound effect becomes so severe that the person not only becomes extremely nervous, but their nervous system becomes so over-stimulated that medical intervention is needed to prevent going into a seizure and even dying.

Look at a drug at the other end of the spectrum, cocaine. Alcohol and opiates relax, but cocaine stimulates us, leading to feelings of exhilaration and euphoria. This would be all good and fine if the story ended here, but it does not. Individuals who have used cocaine repeatedly find that they experience the rebound effect as well. Cocaine users have brief periods of euphoria, followed by longer periods of depression and the inability to experience pleasure. I am not an expert on the neurochemistry of addiction, but my understanding is that basically cocaine users burn up all their "happy" neurotransmitters in a few short minutes and are left impoverished for days. Penny wise, pound foolish. This is why we have the PLEASE skill of Avoid mood altering drugs. It is not about being a goody-goody. It is about choosing the pound over the penny. Remember, with current US to UK exchange rates, that is a ratio of 126 to one.

PLEASE: BALANCED SLEEP—WHO IS THE THIEF?

In my private practice, I have come to find that I work with a lot of younger people who stay up fairly late into the night, using social media, texting, playing online games, and the like. Many of these persons will stay up to one, two, three, even four in the morning, then are under pressure to get up and go to class or to work by 8:00 or 9:00 am. They noticed that they're in a bad mood during the day, but don't make the connection that it was in large part due to not getting enough sleep the night before.

Other people that I work with will stay up just as late, perhaps as late as 3:00 or 4:00 am, and then as a result may sleep until noon or later. Many of these folks struggle with depression. They feel lethargic, unmotivated, and do not get as much pleasure from everyday activities as they should. Likewise, some of these folks do not make the connection to their sleep life.

Our world has changed radically in the last 150 years. Before this time there were no electric lights. When the sun went down, people went to bed and fell asleep. Our bodies evolved over millions of years; they are adapted to our physical environment. But with the invention of the electric light bulb, and the many gadgets in its wake, suddenly our environment has changed. If we attempt to live in a way that our bodies are not adapted for, serious mood problems result.

The PLEASE skills help us take care of our mind (emotional life) by taking care of our body. Our body needs sleep, if we don't get the right amount of sleep, our body will feel like shit, and our moods will follow suit. If we sleep too much, we will feel lethargic and listless. If we sleep too little, we will feel tired and irritable. Balanced sleep includes having the right amount of sleep: neither too much nor too little.

But it is also advantageous to sleep at the right time, if possible, at night. Scientific research points to the need for sunlight to create positive mood. Almost all of us are aware that at the darkest times of the year (December and January in the Northern Hemisphere), we are more at risk to feel lower in mood, and are at risk to slip into malaise and perhaps depression. We need sunlight and we need it in large amounts. There is nothing intrinsically wrong with being on social media or playing Fortnight late at night, except that it makes us miss out on either having enough sleep or enough sunlight. Author Peter Guralnick points out in the last ten-plus years of his life, Elvis Presley rarely was awake during the daytime and stayed up all night (Guralnick, 1999). It is little wonder that this tremendous artist died at age 42 with 15 substances listed in his autopsy.

Author Pedram Shojai has a list of tips on how to have balanced, restful sleep that soothes our minds and nourishes our spirits (Shojai, 2016). These include no caffeine after 2:00 pm at the latest (preferably caffeine stops at noon), no paying bills or doing stressful activities in the bedroom, the bedroom is for sleeping and making love, keep the TV and other electronic devices out of the bedroom, and keep your bedroom cool & dark. Sleep researchers point to these and other important factors as necessities for getting our sleep back on track (Edinger & Carney 2008).

My fear in writing this portion of my book is that some of the readers may think of me as a strict parent or school teacher, lecturing the readers that they "should" go to bed. That is not my intent. My intent is to show that when any of us short change ourselves in regards to sleep, we become the thief who robs our self of a positive mood.

PLEASE: EXERCISE FOR OPTIMAL MOOD

The last of the PLEASE skills is Exercise. Exercise is important for creating a positive mood and decreasing vulnerability in a number of ways.

First, as most people now know, exercise increases endorphins, neurochemicals that produce a sense of happiness, peace, and contentment. The term endorphin is actually a contraction of the phrase in "endogenous morphine" because endorphins are actually fairly similar to opiates like heroin, Vicodin, Percocet, and morphine. The latter drugs of abuse actually do their work at the endorphin receptor sites in the brain, mimicking endorphins. People use heroin, Vicodin, and morphine because they produce feelings of happiness, contentment, and peace. The catch is these drugs only work for a few hours, then they wear off. If one merely returned to baseline, heroin, Vicodin, and the like would not be problematic, but this is not the case. The man-made substances cause a rebound effect when they are eliminated by the liver, leaving the user feeling depressed and nervous, with a sense of discontent; the user keeps having to up the dose to diminishing returns as the body becomes more and more adept at eliminating these drugs from the bloodstream.

However, there are no rebound effects with endorphins. We don't experience the diminishing returns (which addiction specialists call tolerance). When we use exercise to produce endorphins, we feel better. As Forrest Gump would say, "That's all I got to say about that."

There is more to say about the psychological and emotional benefits of exercise. In his book *The Urban Monk*, Pedram Shojai (2006) says:

> ...for thousands of years, life was about movement (p. 98). We ran to catch prey, and we ran to avoid being prey. We climbed over the terrain in search of vegetables, berries, nuts and mushrooms. We chopped wood and carried water. We had no furniture to support our bodies when sitting down and so we sat in a way in which we supported our weight, strengthening what we now call our core. We used our whole body all day. That is the way that we evolved over millions of years, with all of this physical activity strengthening our bodies. Now that most of us live very sedentary lives, the bodies ache because we are not getting enough physical activity to stay in good condition.

As such, our bodies feel bad. When our bodies feel bad, this is what we call in DBT a Vulnerability Factor.

Shojai points out the Surgeon General of the United States recommends a minimum of one hour of cardio exercise per day, but less than 5 percent of Americans get even 30 minutes of daily physical activity. This may constitute "the mother of all vulnerability factors."

This is just common sense; it is easier to feel psychologically good when we feel physically good.

REFERENCES

Abbate, A, Ashton, M, Berman, B, Burton, J, Fleming, K, & Melniker, B (Producers), Lord, P, & Miller, C (Directors). (2014) *The Lego Movie* [Motion Picture]. United States: Warner Bros.

Basco, M R. (1999) *Never good enough: How to use perfectionism to your advantage without letting it ruin your life.* New York: Touchstone Books.

Beaumont, C (Writer) & Brahm, J (Director). (1960) *A Nice Place to Visit* [Television series episode]. In. R Serling [Executive Producer], *The Twilight Zone.* United States: Cayuga Productions & CBS Television Network.

Beck, J S. (2011) *Cognitive therapy: Basics and beyond.* New York: Guilford Press.

Brubaker, J D (Executive Producer), & Kaufman, P. (Director). (1983). *The Right Stuff* [Motion Picture]. United States: The Ladd Company.

Ellis, A. (1962) *Reason and emotion in psychotherapy.* Secaucus, NJ: Lyle Stuart.

Finerman, W, Newirth, C, Starkey, S, Tisch, S (Producers), & Zemeckis, R (Director). (1994) *Forrest Gump* [Motion Picture]. United States: Paramount Pictures.

Gottman, J M. (1997) *Raising an emotionally intelligent child.* New York: Simon & Schuster Paperbacks.

Greenberg, L S & Paivio, S C. (1997) *Working with emotions in psychotherapy.* New York, Guilford Press.

Gross, J J (Ed.). (2007) *Handbook of emotion regulation.* New York, NY, US: Guilford Press.

Guralnick, P. (1999) *Careless love: The unmaking of Elvis Presley.* Boston: Little, Brown, and Co.

Hayes, S C, Strosahl, K D, & Wilson, K G. (2012) *Acceptance and commitment therapy: The process and practice of mindful change* (2nd ed.). New York, NY, US: Guilford Press.

Linehan, M M. (1993a) *Cognitive-behavioral treatment of borderline personality disorder.* New York, NY, US: Guilford Press.

Linehan, M M. (1993b) *Skills training manual for treating borderline personality disorder.* New York: Guilford Press.

Linehan, M M. (2015a) *DBT skills training: Handouts and worksheets.* New York: Guilford.

Lombardo, J. (2005) *A fire to win: The life and times of Woody Hayes.* New York, Thomas Dunne Books.

Lynch, T R. (2018) *Radically open dialectical behavior therapy: Theory and practice for treating disorders of overcontrol.* Oakland, CA, US: Context Press/New Harbinger Publications.

Mueser, K T, Noordsy, D L, Drake, R E, & Fox, L. (2003) *Integrated treatment for dual disorders: A guide to effective treatment.* New York: Guilford Press.

Muller, R. (1964) *Rudolph the Red-Nosed Reindeer.* Videocraft International, Ltd.

Panksepp, J. (2005) *Affective neuroscience: The foundations of human and animal emotions.* New York: Oxford University Press.

Parks, C C. (1967) *Somethin' Stupid.* Greenwood Music Corp.

Ramis, H (director) & Kenney, D. (1980) *Caddyshack* [motion picture]. Warner Brothers Pictures.

Shojai, P. (2016) *The urban monk.* New York, NY, US: Rodale Inc.

Spielberg, S (director), Zanuck, R D, & Brown, D (producers). (1975) *Jaws* [motion picture]. Universal Pictures.

Wampold, B E & Imel, Z E. (2015) *The great psychotherapy debate: The evidence for what makes psychotherapy work, second edition.* New York: Routledge, Francis & Taylor Group.

Webb, J. (1951) *Dragnet* [television series]. Mark VII Limited.

Distress Tolerance, Part One

Chapter 5

DISTRESS TOLERANCE—WHAT IS IN A NAME?

When introducing the Distress Tolerance module, I point out how much sense the name of the module makes. I will break it down, helping group members think through what these words mean. I ask group members, "How many of you feel overwhelmed?" To date, I have yet to have anyone not raise their hand. Everyone experiences stress, including when it escalates to the point of being distress.

My understanding is that the word *tolerance* came from the vocabulary of engineers. For example, when engineers design a bridge, they calculate how much weight the bridge can *tolerate*, meaning how much weight the bridge can bear before it breaks down. Stress is like that: if we can bear up under it, we're able to tolerate it, if we can't, it breaks us down, resulting in painful emotions and self-defeating behavior.

I also emphasize another aspect of what "tolerance" means. Sometimes people believe the myth that they should not *have* to tolerate stress, believing if they're living their life the right way, they won't have any stress. This belief is not true on the planet we live on; there will always be stress and our task is to tolerate it.

On occasion, people will try the Distress Tolerance skills and find their stress level lowered, but not eliminated, and conclude that the Distress Tolerance skills are not worth the effort. The truth is, if we can get our stress level under a score of 70 out of 100 on the Subject of Units of Distress Scale, we can avoid Crisis/Problem Behaviors that that make our life worse, turning it into a labyrinth of suffering and chaos. As you will see, when you can get your level of emotional distress under 70 on the 100 point scale, your ability to avoid behaviors that wreck your life is improved dramatically.

DISTRESS TOLERANCE MODULE—THE IRONY OF THE NAME

Mindfulness, Interpersonal Effectiveness, and Emotion Regulation are three modules that will make your life better. However, I tell my DBT students that the goal of the Distress Tolerance module is not to make your life better. So why do we work on Distress Tolerance skills? We do not work on Distress Tolerance to make our lives better, we engage in Distress Tolerance skills to *prevent* making our life *worse*.

Think of times you have engaged in self-defeating behavior. What if you could magically erase these behaviors from the last six months of your life? How much better would your life be? Sometimes the secret of having a good life is not about making it better, it's about preventing ourselves from making it worse (Linehan, 2005a, 2005b).

Crisis (or Problem) behaviors give us quick, short term relief from stress. But Crisis/Problem Behaviors create more stress in the long run and lead to a more impoverished life. Examples of Problem or Crisis Behaviors include self-harm, substance use, other addictive behaviors (gambling, compulsive shopping, compulsive sexual activity), or engaging in destructive behavior such as breaking things, physical fights, and making insults. These behaviors do give us temporary relief, but they make our life worse in the long run.

If you have ever felt that you are your own worst enemy, it is probably because of the Crisis Behaviors you engage in to relieve your stress. We engage in Crisis/Problem Behaviors because we know of no other way to relieve our stress. The Distress Tolerance module will give you the skills to avoid engaging in Crisis Behaviors and break the downward spiral of your life.

If you prevent yourself from making your life *worse*, your life will become *better*.

CRISIS BEHAVIOR/PROBLEM BEHAVIOR—POISON IVY METAPHOR

One of the goals of the Distress Tolerance module is *freedom*. The freedom we seek is freedom from the tyranny of dependence on Crisis/Problem Behaviors to ease our stress (albeit briefly) when overwhelmed. Problem Behaviors can become addictions. The more we use Crisis Behaviors to ease our distress, the more of them we will need to use in order to get relief, leading to increased craving for the Crisis or Problem Behavior until the cycle runs out of control.

A Crisis Behavior (I prefer the term Problem Behavior) is one that creates quick, easy relief in the short run, but makes our life worse and more stressful in the long run. The metaphor I use to teach this involves poison ivy. I ask my group, "If I have poison ivy and it itches, will scratching it make it feel better?" Yes, of course scratching the poison ivy will make it feel better, but only for the time that I am scratching. Yes, it gives me instant relief, but I've just spread the poison ivy over a larger area of my skin.

Problem Behaviors like self-harm, abusing substances, engaging in aggressive behaviors, or procrastinating do give instant relief, but only for the period that you are doing them. Most people who engage in these behaviors for relief do realize they are becoming enslaved to these habits, and hate being subjected to the servitude to the problem behavior.

Resisting the urge to "scratch" is not easy. But just like with poison ivy, the longer you go without engaging in the Problem Behavior, the less intense the urges to "scratch" will be.

Also of note, the Distress Tolerance skills you will study will reduce the intensity of the "itching," (sort of like

Calamine lotion or cortisone cream will *reduce* some of the itchy sensation). This is good news. But there will be some remaining urge to scratch. It remains your responsibility to refrain from scratching.

CRISIS/PROBLEM BEHAVIOR: LOAN SHARK METAPHOR

Crisis/Problem Behaviors give us short-term relief from stressful emotions. Everyone has one or two (at minimum) of these behaviors. These might include cutting yourself, excessive gambling, alcohol or drug use, having a rage-filled blow up, or perhaps the sneakiest of all Problem Behaviors, avoidance/procrastination. Quick and easy relief—what's the problem?

The problem with Problem Behaviors is they are like going to a payday loan company, or even worse, a loan shark. Yes, you get quick, easy money, but the price you pay is hefty. The interest on this money will make your life much more stressful in the long run, even though it gets you through the immediate crisis.

The book *Healing the Shame that Binds You* (Bradshaw, 1993) has an excellent diagram that shows how a painful emotion leads to the urge to engage in a Problem Behavior. If we give in to the urge, we do get the quick relief, but soon the painful emotion comes back a little stronger, accompanied by feelings of guilt and shame. The Problem Behavior also leads to an added negative consequence. For example, calling in sick to work to get drunk leads to more problems at work, and in turn, more stress. The person that does this has just dug themselves into a deeper hole. A primary goal of the Distress Tolerance module is to break this downward cycle and gain freedom from the loan shark of Crisis Behaviors.

CRISIS/PROBLEM BEHAVIOR: WALK THE LINE

Marsha Linehan uses the term "Crisis Behavior" to describe a wide range of maladaptive actions such as self-harm, substance abuse, aggressive behavior, and procrastination, all of which are ineffective ways to deal with distress. Cutting oneself and staying in bed all day may seem like very different behaviors, but they are both ineffective ways to cope with stress. All Problem or Crisis Behaviors are more common than initially meets the eye. A Crisis or Problem Behavior is a behavior that gives us quick relief in the short run, but in the long run makes our life a bigger mess and actually increases the amount of stress or distress that we're feeling. The goal is to break the cycle of dependency on the problem behavior and thus prevent piling up more stress in your life.

The film *Walk the Line* (Keach, Konrad, & Mangold, 2006) was nominated for four Academy Awards (Reese Witherspoon won Best Actress for her portrayal of June Carter). The movie accurately displays how crisis or problem behaviors can develop, how they "scratch the itch" of the urge, giving momentary relief, but dig us into a bigger pit of distress.

In the film, Johnny Cash has a crush on another singer, June Carter. After finishing one of his hit songs on stage, he calls off-stage for June to come out and sing a spontaneous duet they had never rehearsed. Cash ignores her facial expression of disdain and exasperation (note how he is ignoring her emotional reaction; he is being the opposite of mindful). When she finally relents and joins him on stage, he suggests a song that she recorded with her ex-husband, "Time's a-Wastin'." Again, Johnny ignores her nonverbal communication (she does not want to sing this song) and she also tells this to him directly, saying "no!" Cash cues the band, the song starts, June reluctantly complies. But then Cash kisses her during an instrumental break, and June runs off stage in tears.

Cash chases June off stage, and finds her weeping in her dressing room. She tells Cash to leave her alone. Back in his dressing room, Cash is feeling a flood of emotions including embarrassment, shame, rejection, and anger. His distress is at the top of the SUDS scale, the Crisis/Problem Behaviors begin. First, he breaks a fishing pole that he used on tour, then he smashes his expensive Martin guitar (worth about $2,000 in 1960) to shreds. Still overwhelmed with agitation, he pulls the handles off the sink then rips the whole sink off the wall. Still jacked up, Cash then swallows a handful of pills (amphetamines or barbiturates), washing them down with a beer. This scene in the movie portrays how these behaviors began digging Johnny Cash into a deeper and deeper hole, beginning in the late 1950s and cresting in the late 1960s. One or two pills became dozens a day and the charges from damaged hotel rooms, wrecked cars, and even a forest fire he started when high put the star into financial problems in the late 1960s. Only when he quit the drugs as well as the other destructive behaviors was he able to rebuild a life worth living.

The example of Johnny Cash illustrates Crisis/Problem Behaviors because he is someone most of us can relate to. He did not have bad intentions. Like many of us, he encountered trauma and hardship early in life. He became so overwhelmed with painful emotions that he experienced the urge to do destructive things that gave him some momentary relief. Only by acknowledging how destructive his behavior was and seeking the help of family, friends, and mental health professionals was he able to break the cycle.

Later in the film, when Cash finally detoxes off of drugs, he experiences remorse for the many harmful and damaging things he has done and the people he has hurt. In a touching scene, June Carter tells him he is not a bad man, and he now has a second chance to make things right. The Distress Tolerance skills allow us to do just that: stop the cycle of destructive behaviors, tolerate the distress, then, when the storm has passed, go back to building a life worth living.

AMBIVALENCE ABOUT REFRAINING FROM CRISIS/PROBLEM BEHAVIOR—TAKING OFF THE TRAINING WHEELS

Most people struggle with refraining from or stopping Problem Behaviors. Though the Problem Behavior produces obvious negative consequences (unsightly and embarrassing scars, hangovers, DUI's), they also have desirable effects (quick relief from intense emotions). It is not surprising that part of you desperately wants to stop the Problem Behavior, while part of you desperately clings to the Problem Behavior. Having others angrily admonish you to "just stop it!" probably does not help, because it does not address the ambivalence about the behavior.

Your DBT therapist understands that giving up a Problem Behavior will be a difficult period for you, much like when a child removes the training wheels from their bicycle. This process can be scary, and it may not go entirely smoothly. Like a child, we may long for the predictability and stability of the training wheels. On one hand, your Problem Behavior protected you from experiencing emotional pain, but on the other hand, it does make your life worse. We know intuitively that the training wheels need to be removed.

By joining a DBT group, you have decided to take the courageous route of taking your training wheels off. Don't berate or shame yourself for using them all those years. Giving up training wheels may initially raise your anxiety level, but don't assume this means it will turn out badly. If you fall some, don't assume that you are inept or can't do it. Get back up. Your DBT therapist will be a supportive parent, encouraging you to get back up, helping sooth your pain, and praising you as you make progress.

RECOGNIZING THE STRESS THAT BEGS FOR PROBLEM BEHAVIOR RELIEF

All DBT modules are built on Mindfulness, including Distress Tolerance. For Distress Tolerance skills to work, you have to recognize (be mindful of, aware of) the stress rising. This is the story of a person reaching for his Problem Behavior at a time when his stress level was most likely at its highest. I will not mention this person by name, though his situation was fully documented in the media.

Decades ago, an NFL team was about was to play in the Super Bowl. This team had a tremendous offense, including a fullback who was not only great at running with the ball, but also excelled at blocking for the other running backs and creating fakes that led to wide receivers becoming wide open. This player had struggled with cocaine addiction and had been suspended twice from the NFL, once for an entire season. He stayed clean during the entire next season, passing three drug screens a week. His contributions helped his team to the conference championship that year by scoring two touchdowns in the playoffs.

Unfortunately, the fullback then relapsed into using cocaine, the night before the Super Bowl, less than 24 hours before kickoff. As such, he became ineligible for the game, and his team narrowly lost by four points. Fans of the team were irate; why would the fullback get high the night before the Super Bowl, blowing it all? Of all the times one could go off the rails, why this night?

This is purely conjecture on my part, but if I were playing in the Super Bowl, my emotional status the night before the game would be one of extreme anxiety. Sure, there would be excitement, too, but it would be mixed with nerves; who wouldn't feel this? Did the player understand and anticipate the normal rise in anxiety before an event of this magnitude? Did he realize it would be a trigger to use, not to party, but to seek relief from the high anxiety associated with playing in the Super Bowl?

This illustrates why Mindfulness of our emotions is so important. If we are not aware of what is going on inside, all the Distress Tolerance and Emotional Regulation skills and techniques in the world will not help us.

Earlier in the year, the team's head coach had suggested the player see a psychiatrist for some problems he struggled with. Unfortunately, the player declined (Cincinnati Enquirer, January 23, 1989). Perhaps the psychiatrist would have taught the player to be more mindful of his emotional processes, and the relapse could have been averted. But we will never know.

All of us have stressful times, all of us have Problem Behaviors that can give us quick relief from stress, but make our lives much worse in the long run. The Distress Tolerance module helps us realize when our stress level is going up, and what to do to prevent the problem behavior.

STOP SKILL: PROCEED MINDFULLY

One of the rules of both checkers and chess is that once you take your hand off of the checker or chess piece, your move is officially over. It is perfectly acceptable to move the piece with your hand and look at how the situation on the board might play out, then pull the piece back to the original position and reconsider another move. Once you take your hand off of the piece, your move is final. You can't undo it.

The STOP skill (Linehan, 2015, p. 327) is basically the same thing. Before you engage in a Problem Behavior, this skill has you first Stop, Take a step back and Observe the situation, think through the consequences of each potential move, then Proceed Mindfully (rather than mindlessly). This saves you from then saying, "OMG, I wish I had never done that!" Once you take your hand off the checker or chess piece, there are no do-overs. These games mimic life, teaching us to Stop, Take a step back (so we can see the whole chess board), Observe the situation, then Proceed Mindfully rather than mindlessly. Remember that a major objective of the Distress Tolerance module is to avoid making regrettable "moves".

PROS AND CONS: JOHNNY CASH AND BONO

Author Robert Hillburn, in his biography of Johnny Cash (2013), tells an interesting story about Cash and Bono of the band U2. U2 was on tour in the United States, and they wanted to visit Cash, whom they greatly respected. Johnny and his wife, June Carter Cash, invited Bono and AdamClavton to have a meal with them in their home in Nashville. The meal was served, and Johnny invited everybody to join hands as he said grace, thanking God for the meal, their friends, and so forth. When Cash was done with the prayer, he said "Amen," but then he looked up, looked directly at Bono and said, *"but I still do really miss the drugs."*

Using the Pros and Cons skill (Linehan, 2015, p. 328), allows us to look at both the adaptive/positive aspects of a negative behavior as well as its negative consequences. Looking fully at what we're giving up allows us to be more honest with ourselves. There's part of us that does want to engage in the Problem Behavior, otherwise it would not be an issue. There is a lot more to be said for giving up the Problem Behavior, but we will miss it from time to time. Acknowledging our fondness for the Problem Behavior helps us to realize that there will be times when we're tempted to pick it back up. Being forewarned is being fore-armed.

I also believe looking at all the pros of engaging in a Problem Behavior is necessary so that we can go through sort of a grief process when we give it up.

TIP SKILLS—THE PARABLE OF THE EXCITED DOGS

Hear ye the parable of the excited dogs. Whenever my wife, sons, and I get the leashes to walk our two dogs (Cubby and Jay-Hey), they become so excited that their whole bodies rock back and forth. Their tails and whole bodies are wagging back and forth with such excitement that we cannot get their Invisible Fence collars off and the leases on. Sometimes it will take up to the three minutes to get them to sit still enough for us to actually get them on the leashes.

Humans experience a similar physiological surge when experiencing strong emotions, especially when accompanied by stress. Our whole body is so jacked up it makes executing our next step a clumsy affair. The first step in effective coping is to physiologically calm ourselves down. Perhaps you have felt like Cubby and Jay-Hey, except the emotional overload that you feel in your body is unpleasant (fear, anger, hatred, etc.) This is where use of the TIP skills (Linehan, 2015, p. 329) is crucial.

TIP skills allow us to calm our body down enough to get back into Wise Mind. When our whole body is jacked up, it is next to impossible to think calmly and Wise Mindfully.

WISE MIND ACCEPTS—PUT YOUR FOCUS ELSEWHERE

The Wise Mind ACCEPTS skills (Linehan, 2015, p. 333) are about distracting yourself from the source your stress/distress. There are times when focusing on your stressor is simply not effective, and actually makes things worse. Take the example of having taken an exam, but having no idea how well or poorly you did. You are waiting to get the graded test back. Brooding over what your grade will be does nothing but increase your stress level. It adds no points to your grade, yet we act in an almost superstitious fashion as if this mental ritual could magically add points to our test score. In reality, stewing over something that we have no control over is detrimental to our psychological and physical health. If we worry a moderate amount *before* the test and it motivates us to study, worry is functional. Worrying *after* the test only puts us at risk for temptation to resort to a Crisis/Problem Behavior, and thus serves no useful function. It is time to distract yourself, to put your focus on something other than the test and what grade you will receive.

I learned a trick in my freshman public speaking class to deal with the fear of public speaking. People directly looking at me while I spoke made me very anxious, so my professor suggested that rather than look people in the eye, I could just look one to two feet above their head. Doing this made it appear that I was making eye contact, but it allowed me to avoid looking at the trigger for my anxiety.

This is the strategy behind the Wise Mind ACCEPTS skills; put your focus somewhere other than on what creates your stress.

WISE MIND ACCEPTS—THE VALUE OF DISTRACTION

Peter Guralnick, in his biography of Elvis Presley titled *Last Train to Memphis* (1994) tells an interesting story about a 19-year-old Elvis getting his first record played on Memphis radio for the very first time. Elvis's 45 RPM record *That's Alright Mama/Blue Moon of Kentucky* was being played by local disk jockey Dewey Phillips. Radio listeners embraced the record like nothing they had ever heard before, and were calling the station to hear more about this local phenomenon.

Phillips contacted Elvis's record company, who gave Elvis' home phone number to him, and he called Elvis' parents. Phillips wanted to interview Elvis on the air right away, and so his parents went to the movie theater where the young star was, walked down the aisles until they finally found him and directed him to the station. When Elvis got to the radio station, he became extremely nervous, and apologetically told Phillips that he didn't know anything about being interviewed. Phillips replied, something to the effect "Just don't say nothing dirty." Phillips and Elvis chatted for a few minutes, and he seemed to calm down. Then Elvis asked Phillips, when was he going to start the interview? "I just did," said Phillips, and suddenly Elvis broke out in a cold sweat.

This story illustrates how sometimes the worst thing we can do with a stressor is pay attention to it. Directing our minds *away* from the stressor, especially when there is nothing we can do about, it is an extremely valuable skill. Wise Mind ACCEPTS is a set of skills to direct our mind *away* from the stressor.

WISE MIND ACCEPTS: THE FRINGE BENEFITS OF BEING ABLE TO DISTRACT YOURSELF

Developmental psychologists have found that one of the key skills in regulating emotion is the ability to self-distract (Eisenberg et al. 2007, p. 295). The ability to control one's attention, to deliberately look away from the stressor, is what is practiced in the Wise Mind ACCEPTS skills. Your reaction to this idea maybe "I'm no good at that!" This is why DBT puts such an emphasis on practice. I am never good at playing a new song on the guitar the first time I play it. It takes repeated practice.

One additional point about self-distraction with the Wise Mind ACCEPTS skills: research from developmental psychologists also point out that children who learn how to self-distract to the optimal amount tend to be much higher in social competence and well-liked to by their peers. Not a bad fringe benefit!

WISE MIND ACCEPTS—CONTRIBUTING

Distracting our attention away from what is prompting our stress is the focus of the Wise Mind ACCEPTS skills. The following is the story of one of my patients who discovered the C = **Contributing** skill.

My patient was a young college student; he was handsome, intelligent, had a college scholarship, had supportive parents, and was very talented in the Arts. He was very popular, but he had also incurred a major trauma in his teen years. While he worked to overcome the trauma, he became extremely depressed. He struggled through a period of major depression, and I, as a therapist, was having no success getting him out of the depression by pointing to all the wonderful realities of his life. One day, I suggested the he try some volunteer work, perhaps going on a weekend trip with a group of volunteers to help people less fortunate. He glumly left my office. I saw him the following week. When he walked in, his mood was radically improved. Not only was he no longer depressed, but he was very upbeat, cheerful, enthusiastic, and happy. He exclaimed, "Dr Esmail, you are right! I'm going to take a year off of college to go work in an orphanage in Nepal!" I thought his parents were going to kill me.

I continued to see this young man for several months until he left to work with the orphans in Nepal. During our remaining time, I never saw him depressed again. We have remained in contact to some degree for over a decade, and he has never been depressed since that day years ago. Since that time, he has dedicated his life to the service of others, is currently finishing up his graduate degree in a helping profession, and is doing extremely well.

All of us have the need to **contribute**. If we aren't, this might be like a vitamin deficiency that no other nutrient can fill. As such, **contributing** is a very powerful skill, one that not only directs our attention away from stressful prompting events, but that creates happiness in its own right.

WISE MIND ACCEPTS—CONTRIBUTING
SKILL: WISDOM OF AN EIGHT-YEAR-OLD

To combine doing charitable work with having fun, I create and promote "Hootenannys," musical shows featuring a variety of musicians (myself included) with the proceeds from a tip bucket going to a local charity. Recipients of these funds have included an after-school "homework club" (tutoring plus nutrition) for underprivileged children, food banks, and Habitat for Humanity.

One afternoon I was about to begin transporting and setting up the large amount of musical equipment (speakers, amplifiers, microphones) needed for the hootenanny. I had to watch my eight-year-old son Nate, and decided to offer him $5 to be a "roadie," helping me to transport and set up all this stuff. Nate accepted the job and off we went. He asked me about the charity, and I explained it was to help "poor kids" get tutoring and much needed after-school nutrition.

The "hoot" started. Bands were playing, and between a change in artists I went to the mic to announce our charity and point to the tip bucket. As soon as I did the first person to pop up was Nate; he marched down to the front and popped the $5 bill I had paid him into the tip bucket. He had the biggest smile on his face. I was surprised, … and impressed.

Nate intuitively knew something that research in Positive Psychology is documenting (Compton & Hoffman, 2013); having compassion and contributing to another's well-being is good for one's own mood.

Sometimes we cannot change the stressors in our lives. At these times, it can be better to *contribute* to someone else—this creates a sense of empowerment and optimism, ("I am making a difference!"). Paradoxically contributing to others can lower our distress. If you don't believe me, ask an eight-year old.

WISE MIND ACCEPTS—OPPOSITE EMOTION

The E in Wise Mind ACCEPTS (Linehan, 2015, p. 333) stands for **opposite *Emotions.*** When you are extremely sad you should not watch a sad movie, but rather one that is inspiring or humorous. If you're angry as a hornet and you're about to lose control of your anger, watching a violent movie is a bad idea. If you are overwhelmed by fear, don't watch a horror movie, but one that portrays the world as a safe and welcoming place.

I was in graduate school from the mid-1980s through the mid-1990s. Clinical Psychology is a very serious, demanding field of study where a great deal time is spent working with people who have experienced tremendous loss, extreme hardship, and huge challenges. We take the plight of our clients very seriously.

During this period of graduate school, I begin to use the **Opposite Emotion** skill without even knowing it. Much to my surprise, I found myself drawn to watching what was then known as the World Wrestling Federation (now World Wrestling Entertainment). WWF was a huge contrast to the very serious and fact-based world of Clinical Psychology. This was an adventure into the world of the absurd. I would watch George "The Animal" Steele, complete with green tongue, get sidetracked from wrestling his opponent, instead choosing to chew the turnbuckle. Here was The Honky Tonk Man, a dreadful Elvis knock-off, complete with super greasy hair, claiming to be not only the best "wrassler" but the best musician in the world. One time I was talking to a friend on the phone and did not successfully hang the phone up on the hook. As such my friend could not get off of the call, she was stuck listening to me raucously laugh at the WWF for about 45 minutes.

The WWF transported me from the often sad, stressful, and serious world of Clinical Psychology to an absurd world which no one could really take seriously. Talk about relief from distress! Ask yourself, 'what TV show would take me to the opposite emotion when I need it?'

WISE MIND ACCEPTS—PUSHING AWAY

The **P** in Wise Mind ACCEPTS is **Pushing away,** physically, mentally or both. A great YouTube clip (Rodgers & Hammerstein, 2014) from the musical *South Pacific* features of song about a female nurse doing this with a fella she was having trouble with. She uses a metaphor of her own. As she is taking a shower, she tells herself she is going to wash the man out of her hair.

Often when people are in conflict with another person, they have a great deal of trouble just letting it go, and feel the incessant need to always "get the last word in." Arguing with someone who is not really listening is a waste of time.

Sometimes we argue with this person, not in person, but in our head, making ourselves more miserable in the process. Whether in person or in our head, we believe that getting in the last word will somehow magically make things better. In reality, there are many times when we are better served by simply **pushing away**. Perhaps at a later time we can address the situation and find a solution, but not when we are overloaded with distress.

SELF-SOOTHE WITH THE FIVE SENSES

One time, when my younger son Nate was in second grade, he had some very difficult homework. He was extremely frustrated to the point that he began crying and angrily shouted he was not going to do his homework. Reasoning with him did not work. Encouraging him didn't work. Yelling at him definitely did not work.

He continued to cry, and when nothing else would work, I went over and begin to gently scratch his back up and down. I then asked him to try another math problem. I continued to massage his back. The massage calmed him down, and he was able to work through all the problems, finishing his homework in a relatively short time. He then enjoyed the rest of the evening. My wife later exclaimed, "Jimbo, that hypnosis thing you did on Nate was amazing!" I explained it was not hypnosis, I was simply massaging his back.

When we are upset and in great distress, we do not need lectures, threats or sermons. We need to be soothed. If we had good enough parents, they taught us how to do this for ourselves (see John Gottman's book, *Raising an Emotionally Intelligent Child*; 1997). Thankfully for the rest of us there is DBT skills training.

Most soothing, just like in my story above, involves physical sensation that calms down our nervous system. Words are not enough.

IMPROVE THE MOMENT WITH IMAGERY: THE HIPPIE KNEW HOW TO USE IT

In approximately 1970, when I was about 12 years old, the United States was in great conflict about the Viet Nam war: many people wanted us to withdraw from South Viet Nam, whereas many wanted us to continue the fight. During this time of disagreement in American sentiment, I saw a TV movie in which a hippie was drafted into the US Army. When I originally wrote this segment, I did not know the name of the TV movie, but one of the reviewers of this work identified it as *The Tribe*. What I have written here is my memory of the film some 50 years later, and so maybe the details are not exactly accurate.

The film started with the hippie getting his long flowing hair shaved off at the outset of boot camp, and his drill Sergeant being displeased that this unconventional man was now a part of the US Army. But the hippie proved to be a good recruit, defying the Sergeant's expectations.

One scene that was memorable was of the hippie's platoon enduring a grueling strength training exercise. All the men were given two buckets full of sand and were told to hold them out away from their bodies. One by one, each man's arms sank back to their bodies as they were unable to endure the weight and they could no longer withstand the pain. However the hippie excelled at this, holding the buckets out while he was actually smiling. The film portrayed how the hippie was *imagining* his girlfriend, in a bikini, running along the beach as the wind blew through her hair. When the hippie was the only solder left still holding the buckets out, the Sergeant commanded him to stop, but the hippie was so engrossed in the *imagery* of his girlfriend that he did not hear the Sergeant, which angered the Sergeant.

Imagery: the hippie knew how to use it and when to use it. Because the hippie had certainly cultivated through practice, he had great skill in focusing on the imagery he chose. The hippie so Improved the Moment, he had a big smile on his face.

It worked for the hippie, it can work for you!

IMPROVE THE MOMENT WITH IMAGERY—ESCAPING THE CAMEL CLUTCH

IMPROVE the Moment skills begin with Imagery (Linehan, 2015, p. 336). This is a very cool skill because you can individualize it to your situation and to your unique psychological makeup. Many imagery meditations are available online for free and you can find them on YouTube. In these exercises, images designed to bring peace and tranquility are described—beautiful beaches, striking sunsets, lush meadows or majestic mountains. Going to these places in your mind will soothe and calm you.

Other sets of imagery can be inspirational and empowering. Some people, in need of inspiration, will imagine a scene from *Rocky* (Kirkwood & Avildsen, 1976) as he runs up the steps to his theme music, or perhaps Olympian Eric Liddell running to the inspiring music of the film *Chariots of Fire* (Fayed & Hudson, 1981).

You need to choose imagery that speaks to you. I grew up in an environment that was awash in criticism and judgment. An image that speaks to me is from the 1984 professional wrestling championship match between challenger Hulk Hogan and the dreaded bad-guy and reigning world champion, the Iron Sheik. Minutes into the match, the Sheik gets Hogan in his finishing maneuver, the dreaded camel-clutch, straddling his opponent as if he were a camel, pulling his head backward. Nobody had ever escaped the camel clutch and the Iron Sheik had it cinched in, but then the Hulk's whole body began to shake, slowly at first, until Hulk broke out of the hold and pinned the Sheik.

At this moment, you may be astonished. Why would I write about something as campy, non-real, and pedestrian as 1980s professional wrestling? The prior paragraph may do nothing for you. The point is *it does something for me.* When I am facing great pressures, demands, and maybe even a toxic situation, the unreasonable, self-critical, and self-judgmental thinking that I was raised on can come back to life, becoming my own inner Iron Sheik. These judgmental thoughts can bend and immobilize me, much like the dreaded camel clutch. If I think of Hulk Hogan getting his second wind, my strength and resolve return, my adrenaline begins to pump, and I am able to "break the hold" and face the challenge of the moment.

I may be the only person on the planet for whom this image works. And that's okay. Imagery works best when it is individualized. You will benefit from finding the images that help *you* during your times of distress. ***Improve the Moment*** with the ***imagery*** that works for you.

IMPROVE THE MOMENT WITH MEANING

DBT tells us to IMPROVE the moment with Meaning (Linehan, 2015, p. 336). In an article in the *New York Times* (Carey, 2011), the creator of DBT, Marsha Linehan, disclosed that, she too, at an earlier point in her life, suffered from the same set of destructive behaviors and uncontrollable emotions that DBT was designed for. She showed the reporter the tapestry of scars coming from cuts and burns on her arms. She was hospitalized at an institution called the Institute of Living on March 9, 1961 at the age of 16, and eventually she became the resident of the seclusion room on the unit, reserved for the most severely ill patients. She was a girl who attacked herself habitually by cutting her arms, burning her wrist with cigarettes, and cutting her legs and mid-section with any sharp object she could get her hands on. When deprived of sharp objects and cigarettes, she did the only thing she could, which was to pound her head on the floor. Marsha was (erroneously) diagnosed with schizophrenia and treated with Thorazine as well as electroconvulsive therapy. None of these methods helped.

Young Marsha said, "I was in hell," then she made the vow, "When I get out, I'm going to come back and get others out of hell." Eventually she was discharged from the hospital and began taking college courses. She was inspired by the idea that two opposite things were true: a person has to come to a place of acceptance about the problems in their life, and, paradoxically, that acceptance of these realities is the step to change (the beginning of her dialectical perspective.) She decided to test her theory out on patients who were very similar to her, suicidal persons diagnosed with borderline personality disorder.

This became the ***Meaning*** of Dr Marsha Linehan's life, to go back and get as many people out of the same psychological hell as she could. Author Victor Frankel was a survivor of the holocaust and lost his entire family in the concentration camps. Frankl stated that people need meaning or they will perish. Marsha found hers. *You* are next.

IMPROVE THE MOMENT: ON THE WINGS OF A DOVE

This story illustrates how one person combined **Imagery** and **Meaning** to shift her focus away from horrible trauma-based memories and improve her life in the present.

I was a young psychologist 25 years ago, working at a community mental health center. One of my first patients was a person who was horribly abused in her childhood on a continual basis. She would have flashbacks and nightmares of these torturous experiences that tormented her horribly. When these occurred, my patient experienced these memories as if they were happening in real time, in the present. Her torment was immense.

One night, I received an emergency call from my patient, who was considering suicide as the only way to escape the torment she was experiencing in the moment due to flashbacks. I wanted to help my patient, to not only prevent her from committing suicide, but to find some relief from these frightening images. I searched my mind for everything I was taught in graduate school, but in vain. Finally, when I could think of nothing else, I remembered that my patient had told me of her grandmother, a kind and sweet Christian lady who did not have custody of her, and thus could not prevent the abuse. But Grandma did what she could. She comforted her granddaughter in every way she could.

One of the things my patient had talked about was her grandmother singing old religious songs to her, which she found very comforting. One of which was a country song from the 1950s by Ferlin Husky (Ferguson, 1958):

On the wings of a snow-white dove
He [God] sends his pure sweet love
A sign from above
On the wings of a dove

The song was based on the Biblical story of Noah and the Ark:

When Noah had drifted, on the flood many days
He looked for land, in various ways
Troubles he had some, but wasn't forgotten
He sent him his love, on the wings of a dove

The first verse compares Noah's situation to ours:

When troubles surround us, when evils come
The body grows weak, the spirit grows numb
When these things beset us, He [God] doesn't forget us
He sends us his love, on the wings of a dove

The only thing I could think of to do to help my patient on that difficult night was to say, "Remember that song your grandma sang to you?" Of course she did. I said, "Remember how it went?" and I sang a couple of bars. "On the wings of a snow-white dove, He sends his pure sweet love, a sign from above ..." She asked me to sing more of the song, that song that her dear sweet grandmother sang to her decades ago (Grandma was long since deceased). Fortunately, I knew all the verses to the song. When I was done, she asked me to sing it again. She was transported back to remembering the love and purity of her grandmother. No one could take that away from her. I knew she was visualizing her grandmother, and hearing her voice (visual and auditory **Imagery**). The **Meaning** came in part from her inseverable relationship with her grandmother, as well as in the words of the song. When troubles beset my patient, this song reminded her that Grandma and the God her grandma served did not forget her.

Several more times in the ensuing years I received an emergency call from this patient, and "On the Wings of a Dove" was sung again. I saw her several times in the years after I left the agency and she was no longer my patient. She married a wonderful man, and no longer experienced the flashbacks and nightmares. Imagery and Meaning: thank God for the wings of the snow-white dove.

IMPROVE THE MOMENT WITH A BRIEF VACATION

When I got married at age 45, it began a relationship in which I found myself having to explain things I've never had to explain before. One that I had great difficulty with was explaining to my wife why, at times, I would disappear for two to three hours, spending the whole time in a music store when I was not buying anything. To her, this was a mindless waste of time. It didn't help that when she asked me, I really couldn't explain it, other than to so "Uh... because I like to."

As I taught DBT skills groups over the last 15 years, I began to realize I was practicing one of the **IMPROVE the Moment** skills (Linehan, 2015, p. 336), taking a *Vacation*. Going to the music store gave me a reprieve from the pressures and sometimes drudgery of everyday life. DBT teaches that vacations are not limited to week-long trips to exotic resorts. The vacation can be as short as a few minutes or, in my case, an hour and a half in a major music store. There I would find several hundred beautiful guitars and dozens of cool amplifiers and other musical gear. This was probably similar to an art lover going to a great museum such as the Metropolitan or the Louvre. In the music store, there were dozens of Fender, Gibson, Gretsch, Martin, and Rickenbacker guitars, basses, and mandolins, as well as amplifiers by Vox, Marshall, Peavey, and Fender; I was in my happy place. No stress, no pressure, just beauty and tranquility.

Your vacation may be taking your 15-minute break and walking around your office building, listening to the birds. It may be talking to a good friend or escaping into a romance novel. It may be working in your garden, doing a five-minute meditation, or riding your bicycle. The essence of a vacation is leaving the stressful place in your life and going to a place that relaxes and refreshes.

Finally ... I can explain to my wife what I was doing in the music store.

IMPROVE THE MOMENT WITH ENCOURAGEMENT— BE YOUR OWN CHEERLEADER

One of the **IMPROVE the Moment** skills that I love to emphasize is the (self) *Encouragement* skill. When teaching the Encouragement skill, I draw two stick figures on the dry-erase board, the first being a stick-figure cheerleader with a big smile, cheerleader outfit, and two huge pom-poms. I do this to illustrate our need to create such a cheerleader on the inside of our self, one that says, "Let's go, you can do it!" No cheerleader worth her or his salt has only one cheer, but many cheers to keep their efforts diverse and non-monotonous. Furthermore, if you're watching a football game, if the other team scores a touchdown, the cheerleaders do not get deflated. A few seconds after the other team scores the touchdown, the cheerleaders are right back at it, encouraging the team with a fresh set of very peppy chants.

Each of us needs to create this kind of cheerleader inside of us, not necessarily with the pom-poms, but one that does not get discouraged. When we are faced with great challenges and discouragement, the cheerleader may just need to cheer even louder.

The other stick figure I draw has a menacing face and a judgmental demeanor. This symbolizes the voice within you who creates a steady stream of critical and judgmental statements from "you can't do this" to more critical and punitive statements like "I always mess up" and "everybody thinks I'm stupid." Cognitive behavioral therapy refers to this as our negative self-talk. If you are in DBT, it is probable that you have such internal negative self-talk, filled with judgmental and uncompassionate thoughts that criticize, humiliate, demoralize, and deflate you.

The good news is that we do not have to fight this latter nemesis, we just need our cheerleader to cheer louder. Let the critic say what he wants, it doesn't mean any of it is true (though you may have assumed it was true your whole life). This is what the encouragement skill is all about. Somebody has taught you to be your own critical nemesis; DBT teaches you to become your own cheerleader and do whatever it takes to recharge your spirit so you can tolerate the stressful situations that life will throw at you. The mistake many people make is that when something goes wrong, they quit cheering. Go to a football or basketball game and you will see the cheerleaders never stop cheering. When the other team scores a touchdown, the cheerleaders may wait a few seconds, then just start cheering louder. Maybe you have had very few cheerleaders in your life, perhaps none at all. Now is your opportunity to do for yourself what no one else did. **Encourage** yourself.

REFERENCES

Bradshaw, J. (1993) *Healing the shame that binds you.* Deerfield Beach, FL: Health Communications, Inc.

Carey, B. (2011) Expert on mental illness reveals her own fight. *The New York Times.* Retrieved from www.nytimes.com/2011/06/23/health/23lives.html.

Compton, W C & Hoffman, E. (2013) *Positive psychology: The science of happiness and flourishing,* Second Edition. Wadsworth Cengage Learning.

Eisenberg, N, Hoffer, C, & Vaughn, J. (2007) *Effortful control and its socioemotional consequences in handbook of emotion regulation,* James J Gross, Editor. New York, Guilford Press.

Fayed, D (Executive Producer), & Hudson, H (Director). (1981). *Chariots of Fire.* [Motion Picture]. United Kingdom: Twentieth Century Fox, allied Stars Ltd., & Enigma Productions.

Ferguson, R B. (1958) *Wings of a Dove.* Husky Music, Larrick Music.

Gottman, J M. (1997) *Raising an emotionally intelligent child.* New York: Simon & Schuster Paperbacks.

Guralnick, P. (1994). *Last train to Memphis: The rise of Elvis Presley.* Boston: Little, Brown, and Co.

Kirkwood, G (Producer) & Avildsen, J G (Director). (1976) *Rocky* [Motion Picture]. United States: Chartoff-Winkler Productions.

Linehan, M M. (2005a) *Getting through the crisis without making it worse: Crisis survival skills: Part Two: Improving the moment and pros and cons.* Seattle: Behavioral Tech.

Linehan, M M. (2005b) *From suffering to freedom: Practicing reality acceptance.* Seattle: Behavioral Tech.

Linehan, M M. (2015) *DBT skills training: Handouts and worksheets.* New York: Guilford.

Linehan, M M. (2019) *Building a life worth living: A memoir.* New York: Random House.

Radical and Reality Acceptance (Distress Tolerance, Part Two)

Chapter 6

If you glance at the table of contents in Marsha Linehan's *DBT Skills Training Handouts and Worksheets* (2015), you will see only a few pages devoted to Reality Acceptance, Radical Acceptance, and Turning the Mind skills. They comprise only a fraction of the Distress Tolerance module. If you look at the table of contents of this book, you see that I have created a whole chapter for Reality Acceptance/ Radical Acceptance that includes many examples. Compared to the rest of the book, this chapter is disproportionately larger. As I finished writing this book, I asked myself, "why did I do this?" Good question.

First, I wanted to give various examples of how people can face hardships, misfortune, and injustice and still live a life worth living. The following examples include people born with birth defects, who were subjected to amputation, wounded in war, imprisoned for crimes they did not commit, and were subjected to racism. All the persons in these examples *overcame* tremendous obstacles *by accepting the difficult reality they faced.* Sometimes they could eventually change much or all of that difficult reality, in other cases they could not, but they still built a life worth living.

And secondly, I included many examples of Radical Acceptance for the purpose of *inspiration.* No matter who we are, sustaining motivation to accept reality is not easy. It requires effort ... sustained effort. Maintaining this commitment to radically accept reality is like maintaining a campfire. If you want the fire to keep burning, you must periodically feed it with new pieces of wood.

I read a story by motivational speaker Zig Zigler (I wish I could cite the reference, but I read it in my dentist's waiting room). Zigler was travelling on a commercial airliner, and struck up a conversation with the business traveler next to him. "What do you do for a living?" the man asked. "I am a motivational speaker" replied Zigler. The business traveler said, "I used to go to those, but eventually the motivation would wear off, so I thought, what's the point?" "That's funny," Zigler said, "I have the same experience with taking showers, I take them, and eventually I get dirty. That's why I keep taking showers."

Kenny Rogers, in the song "The Gambler," says that, in poker, every hand is a potential winner, and likewise a potential loser, which is an accurate metaphor for our lives. No matter how difficult the realities of our lives, if we accept reality, we can turn our circumstances into a life worth living.

RADICAL ACCEPTANCE: WE WILL ENCOUNTER PAIN, BUT LIFE CAN STILL BE WORTH LIVING

One of the truths Radical Acceptance teaches us is that we will all experience pain, but life can still be worth living. One of the myths that poses danger to our psychological well-being is telling ourselves, "To have a life worth living, I must not experience pain." In reality, rejecting reality causes suffering and misery to accumulate exponentially.

Two movies that are real-life stories of two of the great musical artists of the twentieth century illustrate this truth. *Ray* is about the great R&B genius Ray Charles (Hackford, 2005), and *Walk the Line* is about country superstar Johnny Cash (Mangold, 2005). Both movies won Academy Awards.

Both Ray Charles and Johnny Cash encountered the deepest of tragedies; they lost their beloved brothers to horrific accidents while they were still children, witnessing their deaths. After becoming commercially successful musicians, both Charles and Cash got into trouble when they were exposed to illegal drugs. They began to use drugs (for Ray Charles is was heroin, for Johnny Case it was primarily amphetamines) to avoid the pain they felt when recalling and missing their brothers. Both used drugs as a way of avoiding/ not accepting the pain that would be with them the rest of their lives. By the end of both movies, Ray Charles and Johnny Cash realize that using drugs to avoid pain was making their lives exponentially worse, and began to accept that their life could be worth living even without using narcotics to avoid the pain.

Accepting a painful reality is not easy, but it is less burdensome than incurring the pain PLUS the suffering that is added to it when we reject reality.

A footnote: one of the things that is tremendously helpful in accepting pain is having someone who listens to and supports us, validating our pain without trying to gloss over it. Note that neither Ray Charles nor Johnny Cash had fathers to support them in the acceptance of the pain, while reminding them that life can still be worth living. Cash's father actually blamed him for his brother's death. Your DBT group and therapist are there, in part, to support you in the acceptance of the pain you encounter. One of the things that helps us accept pain is a relationship with a supportive person, such as your DBT therapist, who is willing to listen to your pain.

REALITY ACCEPTANCE: TEACHING POINT— ACCEPTING UNPLEASANT REALITIES AND PAIN DOES NOT EQUAL WALLOWING IN PAIN

One of the very bright graduate students that I supervised years ago, Dr Nikki Winchester, made this excellent point during a DBT group: accepting reality and accepting pain is not the same as wallowing in pain. Let me contrast the two.

Wallowing in pain often includes endorsing the myth that life must be fair for us to build a life worth living. This myth is very anti-dialectical; the truth is our life can contain both painful realities and be worth living, two very opposite truths. Wallowing is when we focus exclusively on the unfairness of life and the pain we are experiencing, acting as if the presence of pain precludes the other truth (that life can be worth living) and that there are other realities in our life that are more positive.

In the Mindfulness module, we learned that Mindfulness practice includes teaching our mind to focus on where we want to direct it. When wallowing, the person's mind is stuck focusing on the pain—the person refuses to direct one's focus to the other side of the polarity, that life can still be worth living and can include times of happiness, love, and meaning. Accepting reality, including the pain ful parts, allows us to balance these two truths, pain on one side, and a life worth living on the other. We can then choose to spend most of our time directing our focus to the "life worth living" side.

RADICAL ACCEPTANCE: JACKIE ROBINSON

Radical Acceptance is accepting that pain is part of life, including our life, yet also know that life can still be worth living. It may be that the amount of pain dealt to us is unfair. We may have to deal with more painful experiences than other people we know. This, of course, *is* unfair. Part of accepting the pain is accepting that life can be unfair; life can give us more pain than others, and/or it can give us pain that we did nothing to merit—for example, a non-smoker can still develop lung cancer.

One of the domains where we can incur pain in is the social realm. The film *42: The Jackie Robinson story*, (Helgeland, 2013) portrays the injustice that Robinson incurred as the first African American to play in baseball's Major Leagues. In his autobiography, Robinson described this endeavor as "a long and bitter campaign" (Robinson, 1995, p. 27). In his first spring training, not only would almost no one talk to Robinson, but his teammates begin a petition to dismiss him from the team, stating they should not be forced to play alongside a "nigger." Many white fans booed him. Sometimes umpires would make blatantly wrong calls, calling Robinson out when he beat a throw to first by several steps. Pitchers were allowed to deliberately throw at Robinson's head (before the introduction of batting helmets), something that had killed one player in the 1940s.

The injustice and emotional pain that Jackie Robinson incurred hit a crescendo when his team, the Brooklyn Dodgers, traveled to Philadelphia to play the Phillies. Phillies Manager, Ben Chapman, came out of the dugout every time Jackie was up to bat, standing close to the batter's box. Chapman chanted, "hey nigger, nigger, nigger …" and peppered Robinson with a variety of humiliating racial insults, such as telling Jackie to throw down his ball cap and dance around, and perhaps the fans would put some money in it.

One of the myths we tell ourselves is "people must treat me fair, or my life will be miserable." Jackie Robinson did not allow the unfair treatment dealt him to derail him from playing a season worth remembering. (He won the 1947 National League Rookie of the Year, and he led the Dodgers to the pennant).

Do people sometimes treat you unfairly? Radical Acceptance can help you rise above the injustice. The injustice will still be painful, and you should try to correct the injustice if possible.

Radical Acceptance will help you press on and build a life worth living. Radical Acceptance can help you become your own number 42, your own Jackie Robinson.

RADICAL ACCEPTANCE: REMEMBERING MY FRIEND DICK

In the summer of 1987, I was 29 years old and in graduate school. I rented a very inexpensive apartment from an elderly gentleman named Dick. He lived in the second-floor apartment, I lived on the third floor. Dick was a man who had a very hard life. He was born with cerebral palsy, which left him partially paralyzed on one side of his body. Dick did not walk until he was eight years old (physical therapy with a stationary bike finally helped him to his feet).

However Dick's Cerebral Palsy was probably not the most tragic or limiting reality in his life. As I got to know Dick over the years, he told me about cruel verbal and psychological abuse he suffered as a child. He told me that his mother would say "I wish you would have died, so I wouldn't have to take care of you and could devote my time to your brother and sisters!" Dick's right arm was partially paralyzed, he could use it, but it did not relax all the way, so it would never hang all the way down like his other arm. Dick told me that his family pushed very hard to have the tendon in the arm severed, so that his arm would drop down all the way and thus look "normal," but he would lose much of his ability to use that arm. Dick also told me that his family were religious fanatics, and so when he entered the normal changes that come with adolescence, his mother started telling him he was a "pervert" because he would get erections.

The day after I moved into the third-floor apartment, I heard Dick yelling. These were cries of hatred, but also anguish and despair. It was gut-wrenching to listen to. Sometimes I could make out part of what he was saying. Usually he was yelling at his mother, who had been dead for decades. I would hear these anguished outbursts several times a week.

And so, I came to understand how Dick had a deep-seated hatred of women. And like many in his generation, Dick, who was white, also harbored not only gender bias, but a great dislike of African Americans. Though I became his friend, I did not condone these two hatreds.

In 1989, Dick fell and broke his hip. After hip replacement surgery, he was sent to a nursing home to rehab. His caregivers were almost exclusively African American women. Now Dick was not only face-to-face 24/7 with the people he disliked the most, but he was very dependent on them. The first time one of these African American women had to give Dick a full-body sponge bath, he not only accepted that this had to happen, but decided to cope with his anxiety, embarrassment, and shame by making a joke. He said, "Have you ever before seen somebody with the body of [the Greek god] Apollo?" The aid burst into heartfelt laughter. Soon, she was calling him "Apollo" and he was calling her "Aphrodite." All the African American women loved to joke and visit with Dick, he was the local celebrity. Dick quickly accepted that these women were not anything like his shaming, rejecting mother. Direct interaction with them demolished his lifelong prejudices.

Dick returned home months later, and I never again heard the anguished shrieks and hateful diatribes that I had heard for the first two and a half years. Dick and I talked about this experience, how it profoundly changed and healed him. To remind himself of this experience he bought a coffee mug that had the words "Class of '89" on it. Dick encouraged me to pass along this story, and so now I am telling it to you.

I think Dick's healing was in large part due to him Radically Accepting the horrible things that had happened to him in childhood. His healing happened after he choose to accept reality as it really was, namely that the African American women were who they were: nonjudgmental, caring, and compassionate. Yes, his childhood was painful and unjust, but he quit adding suffering to this pain by fully **Participating** in the present (Mindfulness skill), using an **easy manner** (Interpersonal Effectiveness GIVE skill), and accepting reality for what it really was.

Thank you, Dick, for teaching me about Radical Acceptance.

RADICAL ACCEPTANCE: MY UNCLE SAM

I have fond memories of my uncle, Edgar "Sam" Starbuck (no, he was no relation to the proprietors of the coffee chain).

During my childhood, my brother and I would get to go spend a week with Uncle Sam and Aunt Norma, and for us it was always one of the coolest weeks of the year. Uncle Sam and Aunt Norma were always great to be around, we had fun playing pool in their basement, going on trips, drinking Pepsis, playing cards, and learning about our older cousins doing things like rebuilding old cars and hot rods, participating in athletics and marching band, etc. Theirs was a happy home that always brightened our spirits.

Let me tell you about the pain in Uncle Sam's life. Uncle Sam served in the United States Army in World War II. One day, he was driving a Jeep and had stowed a heavy towing chain under his seat. A German solider threw a grenade under the Jeep and the man riding with Uncle Sam was killed instantly. The presence of the heavy chain under Uncle Sam shielded him from some of the impact of the explosion, and thus saved his life.

Uncle Sam returned from the War and married his sweetheart, Aunt Norma. But he returned a wounded veteran. Doctors did the best they could, removing as much shrapnel as they could from his leg, but they could not get all of it. My understanding is that Uncle Sam carried some of the shrapnel with him until the day he died. He did have several surgeries during the time I knew him to remove other pieces of metal, which would lead to some improvement. However, from the explosion on, Uncle Sam walked with a pronounced limp. At family gatherings, if we tossed a football or played badminton, so did Uncle Sam, except he could never really move more than one step at a time. At times, I saw him take his boot off, and there were ulcers and red sores that were certainly painful. I have no doubt he was in some degree of physical pain for the last 60 years of his life.

But I never heard Uncle Sam complain. He had a great sense of humor. He always seemed happy (unless he was mad at one of my cousins for not behaving properly or perhaps frustrated when trying to fix a car).

My uncle Sam may have been the greatest example of Radical Acceptance that I have personally known. As Marsha

Linehan states, Radical Acceptance is accepting that pain is part of our life, and yet our life can be worth living.

REALITY ACCEPTANCE: THE LAUREN HILL STORY

In 2014, the story of a sophomore at Mt. St. Joseph University became front page news (Daugherty, 2014) in my hometown of Cincinnati, Ohio. The young woman's name was Lauren Hill. Lauren was diagnosed with a rare form of brain cancer called Diffuse Intrinsic Pontine Gilioma (DIPG). Persons diagnosed with this cancer live usually only a few weeks to a few months after receiving the diagnosis. No one survives this cancer.

Lauren was a member of the Mt. St. Joe University women's basketball team, and one of her life goals was to play college basketball. With the advent of her diagnosis, her goal was to play in a single game. To accommodate this, as well as to accommodate the groundswell of public interest in seeing Lauren play, Mt. St. Joe's first game of the season against Hiram College was bumped up from November 15, 2014 to November 2, and moved to the much larger Cintas Center of Xavier University. Once this shift was announced, the 10,000 seat Cintas Center sold out in less than 24 hours.

Lauren was a spiritual person, and as you may remember, in the IMPROVE the Moment (Linehan, 2015, p. 336) acronym, the M stands for Meaning. In an interview with the Cincinnati Inquirer she stated, "I asked God if I could do anything. I didn't know what He sent me here for. I wanted to know what He sent me here for. Whatever He sent me here for, I'm ready to do." The two things Lauren came away with from this question were the message of reminding us that goodness matters, and to call attention to the public for the need for funding medical research for DIPG.

Choosing to respond to her fatal illness with Radical Acceptance resulted in increased Mindfulness for Lauren. She said, "It's almost like you've been sleeping your whole life, and someone says, 'hey, wake up'." Her mother Lisa stated, "You have to stay in the moment, because if you let your mind wander, if you don't keep it roped in, it can take you to dark places. Why worry about what's down the road when you don't know how long it really is?"

Rather than wrestle with *why* this happened to her, Lauren choose to stay in the present, she choose *what* she would do with her precious time, and *how* she would live. She continued to play with her teammates, and support their efforts on the court. In those few precious and final weeks of her life, Lauren's initial efforts raised over 1 million dollars for medical research into brain cancer. From when she first learned of her brain cancer to her death in 2015 was only a matter of months, but she made this time worth living.

ACCEPTING PAINFUL REALITIES: AN EASIER, BUT NOT EASY TASK

My primary job is working as a psychologist at a state psychiatric hospital. I work with a number of persons, many of whom have either schizophrenia or bipolar disorder. I encounter persons on a daily basis who deny having a major psychiatric disorder, or deny that they were exhibiting symptoms at the time they were involuntarily hospitalized. In the vast majority of cases, what led to the person needing to be hospitalized was that they discontinued their psychiatric medication, denying they needed it (this accounts for perhaps 90 percent of our admissions).

It is a painful reality to discover one has a major mental illness like schizophrenia or bipolar disorder. Discovering this leads to a sense of hurt, wounded pride, anger, embarrassment, and even shame. As such, I always try to exhibit compassion for my clients, all of whom have incurred a misfortune through no fault of their own, just a bad roll of the genetic dice, something that just as easily could have happened to me or you.

At the same time, I observe that the pain associated with having one of these disorders is compounded and magnified by *denial* of this unpleasant reality. I once calculated the approximate number of persons having these disorders in our catchment area as being approximately 60,000 people (about 2.5 million people in our area times the prevalence rate for the disorders). *Why* are these 290 people locked in our hospital, while the other 59,710 persons with the same disorders are out in the community and enjoying their freedom? Many of the 59,710 accept the reality of their need for psychiatric treatment and are thus able to stay out of the hospital.

Accepting reality does not make our life easy, but rejecting reality makes our life exponentially more difficult.

RADICAL ACCEPTANCE: VIKTOR FRANKL

Viktor Frankl, MD was a bright young man of Jewish decent, born in 1905. While in medical school, he organized a special program in his home of Vienna, Austria to counsel high school students, with the result that not a single high school student committed suicide in 1931. He went on to a successful career in neurology and psychiatry.

However, when Dr Frankl was 33 years old in 1938, the Nazis gained control of Austria. Frankl was no longer permitted to practice medicine with Arian (non-Jewish) patients. By 1944, both Frankl and his wife Tilly were transported to the Auschwitz concentration camp, then to a camp associated with the Dachau concentration camp. By the end of World War II, his wife, mother, and brother were all killed in the death camps, with only one close relative surviving, his sister Stella.

After being in death camps, Dr Frankl returned to practicing neurology and psychiatry, he also taught and authored a number of books. His most famous book was originally titled *Nevertheless, Say "Yes" to Life: A Psychologist Experiences the Concentration Camp*, with the title eventually being changed to *Man's Search for Meaning* (Frankl, 1992).

It is obvious that Dr Frankl endured a phenomenal amount of psychological pain in the 1940s, and probably for the rest of his life. Yet he was an example of what Marsha Linehan points out is the central tenant of Radical Acceptance: our life can be painful, and yet we can build a life worth living.

RADICAL ACCEPTANCE: THREE EXAMPLES OF COURAGE

The basic premise of Radical Acceptance and Reality Acceptance is that very difficult, even traumatic things can happen to us and yet we can still build a life worth living. These are two opposites that are simultaneously true. In other words, one must take a dialectical perspective to hold on to both of these opposites. Many people will accept one as true, but not the other. Only when you hold on to both do you have a realistic, workable way of dealing with the world. Denying either side of the polarity leaves us off balance.

Painful and destructive things can happen to us *and* our life can still be worth living. Here are three examples.

Helen Keller was a young and happy girl until, at 19 months old, she contacted a debilitating disease which was probably either scarlet fever or meningitis. The infection caused Helen's brain to swell, resulting in her losing her eye sight and hearing. Helen developed several signs with which she could communicate with one of the neighbor girls. She was put in touch with a physician who recommended a woman named Annie Sullivan to be her tutor. Helen went on to advocate for many causes, including women having the right to vote, the rights of laborers, and entertainment for our military during times of war. By her own account, Helen had a rich and full life in spite of what happened to her.

Steven Hawking was born to a family who loved education and valued it for their four children. Steven went to Oxford to study, but then developed a neurological disease akin to ALS, eventually leaving him in a wheelchair. Despite this, he continued to study at the graduate level, getting a PhD in physics and mathematics from the prestigious Cambridge University. He won many awards as a scientist during his career, and was also given the US Medal of Honor. He authored a best-selling book, *A Brief History of Time* (Hawking, 2017), which explains the workings of the universe in terms that the average person can understand. In spite of his physical limitations, he built a life worth living.

Christopher Reeve was a successful actor making a number of critically acclaimed films such as *The Bostonians, Street Smart* and *The Remains of the Day.* He was honored with the Screen Actors Guild Award and two Golden Globe Award nominations for his performance in the remake of *Rear Window*, originally an Alfred Hitchcock film. He is perhaps best remembered for playing Superman in the movies. On May 27, 1995 Reeve was riding in an equestrian event and was thrown from his horse. His injuries left him a quadriplegic for the rest of his life. From that point on, he had to use a wheelchair and a ventilator to breathe. He died about a decade later. He used his final years as a spokesperson and advocate for persons with spinal cord injuries, advocating for stem cell research to treat these devastating accidents. His dedication to humanitarianism was part of his building a life worth living.

All three of these persons experienced tremendous tragedies, but overcame the obstacles in their path to construct a life worth living. Doing so did not erase all the pain in their lives, nor did it mean that they had no sorrow for what they lost. Rather, it is in spite of such hardships they were able to live a life worth living and reinvent what would become the rest of their lives.

REALITY ACCEPTANCE: THE WRESTLER WHO COULD

Reality Acceptance teaches us that negative things can happen to us and our life can still be worth living. When I was attempting to explain this to my DBT group, I ran across the following story.

Dustin Carter was a five-year-old boy in rural Ohio, when he developed a rare blood disease. The only way doctors could save his life was by amputating both arms at the elbow and both legs at the knee. Can you imagine being a five-year-old boy wanting to run and play with your friends and have this happen?

In seventh grade, Dustin decided he wanted to go out for his school's wrestling team. With support from family, friends, and the school, he begin to wrestle. His senior year, his record was 42–3 and he qualified to wrestle in the state championship tournament.

I know how I would have reacted if I had had Dustin's amputations at age five. I would have told myself, "My life is ruined, there is nothing I could do to be successful." But that's not what Dustin did. Obviously, he did accept the reality of the situation, he was not in denial of his losses. What he did do was use what he still had. That's what Reality Acceptance is.

By accepting reality for what it was and moving forward, Dustin Carter was the master of his fate and the captain of his soul. For more on Dustin Carter's amazing story, check out the articles in the *New York Times*, February 29, 2008, and also *Sports Illustrated*, April 1, 2008.

RADICAL ACCEPTANCE: BRIAN BANKS

Brian Banks was a fast-rising high school football star from Long Beach, California. For reasons unknown, a woman that he "made out with" falsely accused him of raping her. Banks had been recruited by the University of Southern California (USC) for a full-ride athletic scholarship, but was now headed to prison. He spent five years in prison and when he was released, he had to register as a sex offender and wear an ankle bracelet. Few companies were willing to hire a convicted sex offender, so Banks was limited in the choice of employment.

In an interview with *People* magazine (Breuer & Smolowe, 2012), Banks said, "I was never at peace about what happened, but what I had control over was my character and the moral teachings my mother had instilled in me," and that one should "never give up on the things you believe in."

After Banks was released from prison, a private investigator was able to record his accuser confessing that Banks did not rape her, and his conviction was overturned.

Consider what Brian Banks said about this injustice: "I don't hate anybody, my anger left me long time ago." The article noted that Banks, during the interview, was "strikingly free of bitterness when he speaks of the woman."

Brian Banks is a compelling example of Radical Acceptance. He does not gloss over this incident in a Pollyannaish, "everything is beautiful" manner. He stated, "it was like finally the truth has been heard. But damn, look at all I went through." The truth is that if Banks held on to hatred for the accuser, he would be poisoning his own soul. At the same time, he does not deny the incredible injustice that was perpetrated on him. By not clinging to and amplifying his anger into hatred, he has refused to become what psychiatrist Aaron Beck calls "a prisoner of hate."

An ancient proverb states "the person who pursues revenge should dig two graves."

The article concluded that by letting go of anger and hate, Banks was able to enjoy simple small things such as going to the pool or watching kids play football in the park. He said, "I'm just enjoying this moment." Radical Acceptance frees us to do just that.

RADICAL ACCEPTANCE AND HAPPINESS: THE STORY OF MELISSA MOODY

I recommend a documentary film entitled simply *Happy* (Shimizu & Belic, 2011) which documents the discoveries of Positive Psychology on the study of happiness. You can find this on Netflix or another subscriber service, or you can be like the old-fashioned author of this book and buy the DVD.

One section of this documentary is devoted to the story of Melissa Moody. Melissa was a beautiful young woman who, during her high school years, was a beauty contestant and was named one of the top 50 debutantes in the United States of America. She had an almost ideal life, got married, and was raising her children in Texas when tragedy struck. Melissa's sister-in-law was sitting in her truck and arguing with Melissa, who stood outside. The sister-in-law suddenly hit the gas and sped away. Unfortunately, Melissa's hand was caught in the door handle, her sister-in-law did not realize she was dragging Melissa, pulling her under the wheels of the truck, eventually running over her. The wheels of the vehicle went over Melissa head, and though she survived this experience, the accident horribly disfigured her face. The woman who had once turned the heads of many people was now turning their heads in a different direction, as they looked away from her disfigured face, too embarrassed to look at her directly. Even her friends were afraid to talk to her. Her husband descended into problematic drinking and eventually divorced her. To make matters worse, during her recovery, she started to have memories of being sexually abused as a child as she lay convalescing.

Melissa stated that she felt like killing herself, but given that she had children to raise, she could not bring herself to commit suicide. She Radically Accepted that she needed to remain present for her children during their growing years. When she committed herself to this action, things started to improve. The dozens of surgeries she had to reconstruct her face did not return her to her former beauty, but she did begin to have a life worth living again. As she fully accepted the reality of her new look, she met a man at a wedding who was not afraid to ask her what happened to her. She liked the fact that he could talk openly and a conversation ensued. Soon they were dating, and eventually they married.

At the end of the segment, Melissa Moody shares the irony that she is currently happier than before the accident. She works in healthcare, helping people recover from their injuries. Her relationships with her husband and children are deep and meaningful.

Happiness does not come from being able to avoid all misfortunes, but rather accepting that misfortune happens, and moving forward to build a life worth living.

RADICAL ACCEPTANCE: NELSON MANDELA AND INVICTUS

Nelson Mandela was an anti-apartheid activist, revolutionary, and political leader who spent 27 years in various South Africa prisons. He worked hard to campaign for the rights of blacks in their native land of South Africa, joining the African

National Congress, and initially working peacefully to bring racial equality to his native land. However, in 1962 he was arrested and found guilty for leading a sabotage campaign against his government, and was in prison for the next 27 years.

The movie *Invictus* (Eastwood, 2009) begins with Mandela's release from prison, his election as the first black president of South Africa, and to almost everyone's surprise, his efforts to lead Africa to peaceful reconciliation. Rather than seeking retribution against the white minority that had ruled and exploited the marginalized black majority, Mandela expressed no bitterness, did not try to give black South Africans the upper hand, and set an example of blacks and whites working collaboratively. The amazing part of the story is that Mandela was not consumed with vengeance and hatred for the whites, given that he had 27 years of his life taken away from him. Sometimes he was locked in a solitary cell, at other times he was forced to do hard labor. Imagine being separated from your family for 27 years.

The title of the movie comes from the poem that Mandela said gave him both the strength and the mindset to not be defeated by the 27 years of prison with no guarantee that he would ever be released. The last verse of the poem (Hensley, 1875) goes as follows:

> It matters not how straight the gate,
> how charged with punishment the scroll.
> I am the master of my fate,
> I am the captain of my soul.

This poem remarkably captures the concept of Reality/Radical Acceptance in just a few short words. It points out that painful and unjust things happen to us, and yet we are the master of our fate and the captain of our soul. There is no promise that these difficult realities are not painful, yet we still have some control of our destiny.

I suggest that you do yourself a favor and watch the movie *Invictus* (Eastwood, 2009). I prefer to watch it with the English subtitles which help me not lose the dialogue in the midst of heavy British accents. This film can do the two things that I have set out to do in this book, explain the skills (in this case Radical Acceptance), and also provide inspiration for you to fully implement this skill.

RADICAL ACCEPTANCE: BAD LUCK AND LOSING THE CHANCE OF A LIFETIME: JIM LOVELL

Jim Lovell was born in 1928, but tragedy struck when Jim was only five years old: his father died in an automobile accident. Nonetheless, Jim grew up to be a thoughtful and competent young man, becoming an Eagle Scout and eventually graduating from the US Naval Academy. Lovell became a US Navy fighter pilot, then a test pilot, then after not making the cut to be an astronaut for the Mercury Space Program, he did join NASA for the Gemini Space Program. Lovell flew two Gemini missions, then flew Apollo 8, which was the first flight to actually get to the moon and circle it before returning to Earth. Lovell then was reassigned to Apollo 13, and he and fellow astronaut Fred Haise were to land the Lunar Module (LM) on the moon and walk upon its surface. But misfortune struck.

During a routine stirring of the cryogenic oxygen tank in the Service Module, there was an explosion and a fire. Now the Apollo spacecraft (Service Module and Command Module) were disabled. Rather than anticipating that he would walk on the moon in several days, Lovell and his crew were in dire risk of perishing in space due to their disabled spacecraft.

This harrowing situation is depicted in the award-winning film *Apollo 13* (1995), starring Tom Hanks as Lovell (the film is excellent; I highly recommend it). The ingenuity of the NASA scientists on the ground and the courage and intelligence of Lovell and his fellow astronauts Jack Swigert and Fred Haise, (as well as astronaut Ken Mattingly on the ground, calculating how to use their remaining fuel to make it back) lead to a successful "plan B" that used the Lunar Module to propel them back to Earth. They defied the odds by surviving this emergency.

Here is where Radical Acceptance comes in. Once safely back on Earth, did Lovell begin to say, "That explosion should have never happened"? Did he ruminate over the lost opportunity to walk on the moon? Did this create a sense of regret that would negatively color the rest of his life experience?

Here is what Jim Lovell did say when interviewed:

> I'm very much disappointed, just as Fred is, and just as Jack is, that we couldn't complete the mission. We certainly wanted to make a lunar landing ... But this was my fourth space flight, and there are many people in our organization who have not flown, who deserve to fly, and are talented enough to fly. And they deserve a mission.
>
> (Lovell & Kluger, 1994, p. 342, 343)

This misfortune could have negatively tainted the rest of Jim Lovell's life, if he let it. Instead, his attitude was to accept both sides of the polarity: the tremendous disappointment of not walking on the moon and the reality that he did fly in space on four different missions as well as the fact that he did not die on Apollo 13. Lovell titled his book **Lost Moon.** It was a loss. But he did not let the misfortune that dropped into his life eclipse the many wonderful experiences that he did have. Rejecting reality and ruminating on unfortunate, often undeserved events robs us of the ability to enjoy the many positive events and the blessings we encounter in life. Saying over and over "it should have never happened" with anger and bitterness often robs us more than the actual misfortune. One of the saddest things that can ever happen to a parent is to lose a child to death. Yet if the parent is so caught up in the loss that all their mental bandwidth is consumed by it, it can interfere with their ability to be present and connected with their living children.

Explaining dialectics, Marsha Linehan says:

[We] encourage clients to let go of seeing the world in "black and white," "all or nothing ways"....The goal of dialectics is not to get participants to review reality as a series of grays, but rather to help them see both black and white, and to achieve a synthesis of the two that does not negate the reality of either.

(Linehan, 2015, p. 291)

Think of Jim Lovell's attitude. It will help you radically accept your own bad luck ... and enjoy your good luck.

RADICAL ACCEPTANCE: DIALECTICAL APPROACH OF FORREST GUMP

A great example of Radical Acceptance is found in the movie character of Forrest Gump (Finerman, et al., 1994). Forrest grew up with two disabilities: one was that he had lower-than-average intelligence, the second was that his spine was crooked, forcing him to have wear leg braces early in his life. We do not know what happened to Forrest's father, except that he was not in Forrest's life from the time Forrest could remember. Forrest was picked on and rejected by almost all of his classmates. Fortunately for Forrest, he had a mother who helped him accept reality for what it was.

In the film, Forest's best friend is mortally wounded in battle, and asks Forest why this happened. Forest simply says "you got shot.

Throughout the movie Forrest does not reject reality, he simply acknowledges what it is and responds the best he can. When other kids refuse to let him sit by them on the school bus, he just goes to the next seat where he is rejected again until he meets Jenny. When bullies throw rocks at him, he runs. When his commanding officer Lieutenant Dan is severely wounded, Forrest continues to be his friend. When he does not catch very many shrimp, he goes back out the next day and looks again. When Jenny dies from AIDS, he turns his attention to raising their son, "Little Forrest".

The film is poignant because it underscores and illustrates the basic premises of Reality/Radical Acceptance; difficult, painful, and unfair things can happen to us *and* our life can still be worth living.

At the end of the film, Forrest is at Jenny's grave, talking to her. He states he doesn't know for sure which philosophy is correct, do each of us have a pre-determined destiny? Or do we make our own destiny? Forrest says, "I don't know, but I think it could be both."

Radical Acceptance is acknowledging that misfortunes and injustices happen. By not getting caught up in the spiral of asking why or demanding the universe be fair, Radical Acceptance helps us respond by changing what can be changed.

Do we have a destiny or do we make our destiny? Forrest Gump was deemed the town idiot. Yet he was the one who was wise enough to respond with a *dialectical* answer, "I think it could be both." Things happened to him that were beyond his control (his destiny), and he responded with acceptance and wise-minded action (he made his destiny).

RADICAL ACCEPTANCE: DENYING REALITY DOES NOT CHANGE REALITY, A SAD STORY OF A GENIUS

All of us, at times, are tempted to deny reality. We don't want to believe things that are inconvenient truths. However, as Marsha Linehan states in the DBT skills training manual, denying reality does not change reality.

Steve Jobs was the co-founder of Apple Computer and easily one of the true geniuses of the twentieth and early twenty-first centuries, revolutionizing the world of computing and helping to make computers household items rather than the exclusive domain of major companies and government agencies, such as NASA. But as his biographer Walter Isaacson said, "He was good at willfully ignoring inputs he did not want to process" (Isaacson, 2015, p. 453).

In 2003, Jobs was experiencing a great deal of pain in the vicinity of his kidneys, and so his physicians ordered a CAT scan of his kidneys and ureter. By accident, the CAT scan revealed a dark space on his pancreas, and the doctors had very bad news: Steve Jobs had a tumor. In most cases, this would be a certain death sentence, with the person only having a few months to live. However, when the doctors biopsied a few cells, it turned out that Jobs had a very rare form of pancreatic cancer, the only kind that is amenable to treatment. His medical staff became teary-eyed, realizing that they could save his life.

What happened next was that Jobs ignored his doctor's instructions to have immediate surgery followed by chemotherapy. For the next nine months, Jobs chose to treat his cancer only by using natural approaches such as such a strict vegan diet with large quantities of fresh carrot and fruit juice, acupuncture and herbal remedies. He even consulted a psychic. Isaacson writes that, "His friends repeatedly urged him to have the surgery and chemotherapy." Isaacson stated that this was the product of "the dark side of his reality distortion field." One of his close friends said, "I think Steve has such a strong desire for the world to be a certain way that he wills it to be that way." Another friend said, "He has that ability to ignore stuff that he doesn't want to confront." Isaacson pointed out that this ability to deny what others were saying is one of the strengths that allowed Jobs to do what other people thought was impossible in the realm of computer technology. For nine months Jobs continued to deny reality of his need for surgery and chemotherapy, a reality that even experts in the field of alternative medicine attempted to convince him of.

Eventually, as the cancer continued to grow, Steve Jobs did turn his mind back towards reality, and underwent surgery, but it was too late. The cancer had metastasized to his liver. Steve Jobs lived another seven years, but in ill health.

Accepting reality the way it is or denying reality is not a matter of intelligence. If it was, Steve Jobs would have surely undergone the medical treatments that his doctors urged him to. All of us, no matter how bright or dull, have the capacity to engage in willful denial of reality, turning our mind away from accepting truths that are not pleasing to our sensibilities. As Marsha Linehan states in the DBT skills manual, denying reality does not change reality.

RADICAL ACCEPTANCE: PAIN AND MISERY

"Pain is inevitable, misery is optional." I wish I could site the source where I first read this, but I can't. To me, it explains how Radical Acceptance decreases our distress. It does not make life not easy, but it does make life much less hard.

I explain it to my groups by drawing a small circle labeled "pain." Then I draw a much larger circle around the small circle and label this "misery" or "suffering." I explain that everyone in life will experience pain. Radically Accepting difficult realities does not make the pain go away. Rejecting reality does not make the pain go away either, but it does add the bigger circle of suffering to the smaller circle of pain. Struggling against reality acceptance adds the layer of suffering on top of the pain.

Scientific research demonstrates that trying to suppress painful thoughts leads to becoming more anxious about those thoughts (Roemer & Orsillo, 2009, p. 98). Acceptance of our experience, even if it is painful, leads to "subsequent decreases in specific disease symptomology" (Brown et al. 2015, p. 407).

Jon Kabat-Zinn created a pain management clinic in Boston, Massachusetts primarily teaching mindfulness meditation and acceptance. Many of the people he treated reported a reduction in the amount of physical pain as well psychological pain that they experienced. One of the ironies of this is that acceptance of the physical pain actually leads to a decrease in pain. In Kabat-Zinn's second edition

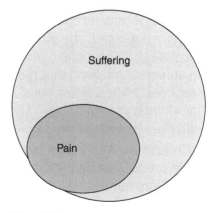

Figure 6.1

of his book *Full Catastrophe Living* (2005), he explains that acceptance is merely acknowledging that the pain exists, without attaching the label "bad" to the experience. When one drops the label "bad," one quits harboring resentment. Harboring resentment leads to clenching one's muscles, which in turn leads to more physical pain as well as emotional angst. Letting go of resistance to pain actually relaxes the body, and thus decreases the pain.

So, there you have it. The choice is yours. You can either have a life with some pain, or a life with the same pain and a lot of suffering and misery added to that. The choice is yours. Reality acceptance is the path to the "pain only" option.

RADICAL ACCEPTANCE AND REALITY ACCEPTANCE

When I first started teaching DBT skills training groups I used the terms *Radical* Acceptance and *Reality* Acceptance interchangeably, not realizing how Marsha Linehan was using the two terms. Finally, it dawned on me why these two different terms were used.

Reality Acceptance refers to *what* we accept. *Radical* refers to *how* we accept it. Think of the What and How skills in Core Mindfulness. Reality is the what, Radical is the how.

Reality Acceptance is not always easy. There are things that are true that are painful, and thus our mind naturally wants to move away from the pain. A friend's husband was killed in a fall while mountain climbing. Despite her family's and friends' encouragement to not view the body, which was horribly damaged, she did choose to look into the casket because she knew she needed this to be able to fully accept on an emotional level that her husband was really dead. Her Reasonable Mind knew what had been reported to her, but Emotion Mind kept turning away from reality. Any of us, faced with the same situation, would have the same struggle.

Turning our Mind back towards Accepting Reality is a five-stage process as defined by Christopher Germer (2009). First, we feel the natural aversion to accept reality; second, we turn towards the discomfort in an effort to embrace reality; third, we begin to tolerate the difficulty of the reality; fourth, we let our feelings emerge. Lastly, we make peace with reality.

The term radical is so over-used (and perhaps misused), that many people don't really get the gist of what the word really means. It comes from the Latin "rad" which means "root." Something that is radical is different clear down to the roots. If you're pulling weeds out of your yard, but don't get the root, soon the weed will be back, just as big and ugly as ever. When we accept something, if we don't do it clear down to the roots, we will not experience the change we seek. What does it mean to accept something clear down to the roots? Dr Linehan points out in the skills training manual that we have to accept things not only intellectually, but at emotional and behavioral levels as well.

RADICAL ACCEPTANCE: TRUST IN REALITY AND RADICAL TRANSPARENCY—A VIEW FROM THE BUSINESS WORLD

DBT directs us to turn our mind towards reality rather than rejecting reality. With that in mind, I would like to tell you a little bit about a person I have read about recently.

Ray Dalio was born in 1949 to a working class family. His father was a jazz musician and his mom a housewife. As a teen he began investing money in the stock market, and in 1971 he graduated from college, then got a master's degree at Harvard Business School. He worked on the floor of the New York stock exchange.

In 1975, Dalio founded Bridgewater Associates, an investment firm out of a spare bedroom in his apartment. In 1981, the firm moved out of his apartment to an actual office. By 2005, Bridgewater was the largest hedge fund in the world, and by 2017, Bridgewater was managing 160 billion dollars in assets. How did Bridgewater achieve so much success in a relatively short period of time? Ray Dalio decided to share the secrets of his success in a book entitled *Principles* (2017).

Dalio states that one key to his success was dedication to a principle he calls Embrace Reality and Deal with it. Later, he admonishes his readers to "trust in Radical Truth and Radical Transparency." How did Dalio come to these ideas? In the book he tells of his life's journey. When he was young, he was much more successful than most of us, and he writes that he thought he knew a lot. However, he shares that in 1993 his three closest associates proposed taking him to dinner "with the stated purpose of 'giving Ray feedback about how he affects people and company morale'" (Dalio, 2017, p. 62). They framed this discussion as "things Ray does well" as well as "what Ray doesn't do so well". Dalio choose to be open to the feedback, and what he learned kicked his leadership up to the next level.

Here is part of what Ray Dalio learned from the process:

> **Understanding, accepting, and working with reality** is both practical and beautiful … Truth—or more precisely, an accurate understanding of reality—is the essential foundation for any good outcome. *Most people fight seeing what is true when it is not what they want it to be.* Radical open-mindedness and radical transparency are invaluable for rapid learning and effective change … *The more open-minded you are, the less likely you are to deceive yourself—and the more likely it is that others will give you honest feedback* … being radically transparent rather than more guarded exposes one to criticism. It is natural to fear that. Yet if you don't put yourself out there with your radical transparency, you won't learn.
>
> (Dalio, 2017, pp. 134–137) (all emphasis mine)

You might ask why I would cite a book on business principles in a book about DBT skills. The answer is, your life is like a business, or maybe I should say your life *is* a business. You are either running your life well, or you are in the emotional and relational "red," not turning a profit, and in danger of "going under." You are at a choice point: do you embrace all of reality, or just the parts you like? Accepting all of reality can be harder in the short run, but for long term success it is necessary.

Your life is a business. How you run it is up to you.

TURNING THE MIND: ACCEPT REALITY—LESSONS FROM A JUKEBOX

Artist, authors, and musicians have been some of the most insightful investigators of human psychology. Country music in particular has a tradition of sad stories. One of the saddest was a huge hit by George Jones entitled "He Stopped Loving Her Today" (Braddock & Putnam, 1980). The lyrics begin with the story of man whose female partner has just terminated their relationship. In the first verse the man, in spite of the breakup, pledges to love her forever, until the day of his death. Throughout the years, the man holds out hope against hope that she will return to him, although nothing in the realm of reality suggests this is a possibility.

Then, the heartbreaking refrain that is the song's title, noting that today, the day of the man's death, is the day he finally stopped loving her. Preparations are now being made for his funeral. The man continued to love the woman for years, perhaps a decade or more, ending only with his death (the song references the couple being together in 1962, the song was released in 1980). Though the song is a work of fiction, no doubt it was based on the observations of the writers Bobby Braddock and Curly Lewis, perhaps a composite of several people they knew who held onto relationships long after the other person broke it off.

If one looks back over the lyrics, the man says from the outset he will love this woman forever, *in spite of* her breaking off the relationship. This man chose to not accept reality, at least on an emotional level, if not intellectual one. No matter what, he vows to keep loving the woman until he dies, rejecting the reality that she has broken off the relationship. The lyrics point to him continuing to hold out hope that she will come back to him even though all evidence points to the fact that this is not likely or even possible. The lyrics point to the man being laid out for a funeral, and the undertaker has positioned his face in a way that the storyteller singing this ballad says it's the first time he saw him smile in years (the mortician posed his face in a smiling position).

This song, which is ranked number 275 in *Rolling Stone* Magazine's Greatest 500 Songs of All Time, reflects what many people do: reject, rather than accept, the reality that the other person has decided to end the relationship and move on. The song also documents how this produces on-going suffering and misery, preventing the man from enjoying his life and possibly finding a new relationship that could be just as fulfilling. Sometimes, people even feel that it is noble, poignant, and even romantic to hold on against all hope.

I am NOT saying that accepting reality in such a situation is easy or something someone can just choose to do like flipping a light switch. On the contrary, our mind keeps wanting to go back to rejecting reality and fantasizing about reunion. Most people who are stuck in this situation realize that they are pining for the relationship and this is actually hurting them, but they feel helpless to change their mental behavior.

Marsha Linehan points to the solution; we have to **Turn our Mind** (Linehan, 2015, p. 345) back to reality over and over. This is a matter of *Willingness* versus *Willfulness*. Are we willing to Turn our Mind back towards reality and tell ourselves this relationship is over? If not, we are consigning ourselves to suffering and misery. I do not want to theorize beyond the data available about the person described in this song, but it does seem he was willfully rejecting reality. Most of us have probably done this when a relationship has been over, but Turning our Mind back to reality and radically accepting reality is the path to building a life worth living. It doesn't mean we don't experience the pain of the loss, but it does mean that we don't compound this with added suffering and misery. Our heart can be broken, and yet we can live and love again, but only if we're willing to *Turn* our Mind and *accept* reality.

WILLINGNESS AND WILLFULNESS: TAKE A LOOK AT YOUR LANGUAGE

One of the psychotherapy models that I was trained in was Gestalt Therapy, which puts great emphasis on awareness (mindfulness). One of the many facets of Gestalt that I find extremely helpful is the emphasis on being mindful of our language (Passons, 1975). A particular case in point is when a person says "I *can't* do that" [stop smoking, arrange a study schedule, abstain from using insulting language when angry at a family member, etc.]. The Gestalt Therapy approach is to have the person who said the "I can't" statement look at whether it is really true ("I can't refrain from demeaning language when I am really mad) or a more accurate statement is "*I won't*" stop the insults, putdowns, etc.

Almost always the person realizes that when they say "I can't," what they really mean is "I *won't*" or "I *am choosing not to*." Having a person observe their language helps them realize that, in actuality, they can make a change, and rather it is a matter of willingness to change. When we cling onto "I can't" statements, we are usually choosing to be willful, and are not willing to admit that we are choosing willfulness.

Sometimes "I can't" statements are true. For example, if someone asked me if I could make the US Olympic Team as a pole vaulter, I would realize that as a 62-year-old man with average athletic ability, "I can't" possibly do that. And often it is understood that when we use the expression "I can't," we are really implying that we could, but doing so would cause great hardship, and so we are choosing not to because we are not willing to undertake a difficult task. For example, I am choosing to not attend a sales party for a product, because I am choosing to go to my son's basketball game.

But much of the time when we say "I can't," we are erroneously deceiving ourselves into thinking we can't, but in reality we are *choosing* to not do something, and this is willfulness.

Recognizing (being mindful of) when we are being willful is the first and crucial step in changing from willful to willing. Often (but not always), when we say "I can't," we are deceiving ourselves.

WILLFULNESS: A LESSON FROM A THREE-YEAR-OLD

When my younger son Nate was only three or perhaps four years old, he had an appointment with a healthcare provider, a chiropractic physician who also specializes in homeopathy and other alternative health practices. I was at my job at the state psychiatric hospital when I got a frantic call from my wife, saying Nate was at his appointment, but was entirely out of control. He would not let the doctor adjust him or even talk to him about his diet. Nate was throwing a tantrum and saying, "I am not going to talk to Dr Pitman! You can't keep me here!" Even though my son was only perhaps four years old, my wife said that she could not physically control him (Nate is exceptionally big and strong, he is on pace to be six-foot-ten). He was creating havoc, disrupting the entire multi-provider office. His tantrum was unending, and my wife told me I needed to clock out immediately and come and intervene.

When I arrived on the scene, Nate refused to see Dr Pitman. I said, "Okay, then we are going home." Nate shouted, "I am NOT going home!" "Well then, I guess we are going to stay here a while," I said, but Nate shouted "I am not going to stay here, you can't make me!" "Well then, let's leave"... "no, I am not going to leave!"

Nate was being the poster-boy for willfulness. No matter what I said, he was not going to do it, even if he contradicted himself a thousand times. But Nate was being no different than any of us. We all do it. It's just that he was providing me with an especially vivid example for this book.

When we become willful, like in the case of three-year-old Nate, all logic goes out the window. Like Nate, we are running solely on Emotion Mind, ignoring what would be in our interest. Willfulness is stubborn. Willfulness is hardheaded and inflexible. The strange thing about willfulness is that we hold on to it even when it is obviously hurting us.

And now, as Paul Harvey used to say, the rest of the story. I picked Nate up, and as he fought and struggled, I put him in his car seat and used the electronic door locks to keep him secured as we drove home. For the first several minutes, he was screaming at me, insisting we go back to Dr Pitman's office. After about three minutes, the gentle vibration of the car put him to sleep, and he slept soundly all the way home.

I put him in bed and he slept for another three to four hours. When he awoke, he was happy, gentle, and loving, and did not remember the episode at the chiropractic office. This illustrates what often maintains willfulness, a vulnerability factor such as being extremely tired, which throws our Emotion Mind into overdrive. Emotion Mind can be illogical and inflexible. A good nap made that all go away.

In case you are wondering how Nate turned out as he grew up, at age 13 (currently) he is a big, powerful young man (he is six-foot-three at age 13), and he is a gentle and thoughtful human being. All of us, especially when overwhelmed and vulnerable, can slip into willfulness. Unlike a three- or four-year-old, we have the ability to turn our mind back to willingness.

REALITY ACCEPTANCE—SUCCESSFUL RELATIONSHIPS

John Gottman, PhD is the world's leading expert on what makes couples happy and successful versus unhappy and dissatisfied. Check out his book *The Seven Principles of Making Marriage Work* (Gottman, 1999) if you are looking for a book to improve your romantic relationship.

One of the myths about successful relationships that Gottman debunks is the idea that if there is a major disagreement in the relationship, this must be resolved for the relationship to be healthy and satisfying. Gottman's research shows that 67 percent of the time, when there is a major disagreement in a relationship, it never gets resolved in one direction or the other (Gottman, 1999). Furthermore, whether this major disagreement is resolved or continues as a disagreement has no bearing on whether the relationship is successful or happy (my wife and I are celebrating our 16th wedding anniversary, and we certainly do not agree on issues ranging from religious differences to differences in how laundry is done).

This fits perfectly with the DBT concept of Reality Acceptance/Radical Acceptance (Linehan, 2015, p. 342). Radical Acceptance tells us that things may be painful or undesirable, and yet we can have a life worth living. Gottman's research points to the fact that we can have a relationship in which we don't agree on everything and yet this relationship is still very much worth having.

If we tell ourselves that our partner has to always agree with everything we do, we are endorsing a myth that undermines our relationship effectiveness.

DENIAL OF REALITY

How does denial of reality start? I am going to tell you a story about one of my sons to explain my understanding.

My oldest son Noah was about two and a half years old. He was wearing a pull-up (disposable diaper) and was successfully using a big boy potty some of the time. As such, some of the time he didn't make it to the potty. One day, I was playing with him and I thought I smelled an accident. I asked him if he pooped his pants, and he said he did not. I asked him if he needed to go the bathroom and he said "no." Minutes later, the smell became so strong that I no longer took his word. "Noah," I said," I am going to look in your pants because I smell poop." Noah emphatically protested, "But I made the poop go away!"

At a young age, we develop an imagination, an alternative world which can often be more pleasing and pleasant. This is where it starts...but certainly not where it ends. We deny reality and make up a preferred fiction because it pleases us. I am thinking of four recent US presidents. One said, "I am NOT a crook," another said, "I did not have a sexual relationship with that woman," another said that he knew another country was amassing weapons of mass destruction and plunged our country into war, and still another lost the popular vote by 2.9 million votes and yet claimed he actually won the popular vote. I think with all four, they talked themselves into believing their fiction because it was more pleasant and less painful than reality.

Three categories of people deny reality in this way: two-year-olds, American presidents, and everybody in between. Remember, as Marsha Linehan notes, *denying reality does not change reality.* If we have an alcohol problem, denying reality does not change our liver enzymes or how out-of-control our behavior becomes when we are intoxicated. If we avoid the unpleasantries of our budget by using our credit card, that does not mitigate the amount of interest that is piling up. If we have only a few relationships, and those are badly damaged, pretending that it's always somebody else's fault not does not help us to build the kind of relational network we want to have.

One area in which I have to turn my mind back towards reality acceptance everyday concerns my intake of food. I once jokingly told someone that I had only two friends growing up, the TV and the refrigerator, and the truth is, I developed a very bad habit of overeating to deal with emotions like boredom and frustration. I like to eat even when I'm not feeling bad. If left to my own devices, I eat too much. Every day I have to turn my mind back to the reality that if I want to stay at a decent weight, I cannot eat in the volume that I want to. I have to turn my mind back towards this reality every day.

Two-year-olds and presidents. You and me. All have minds that wander into the world of make believe. But in reality, none of us can really make the poop go away.

REFERENCES

Braddock, B & Putnam, C. (1980). *He stopped loving her today.*

Breuer, H & Smolowe, J. (2012) *A wronged man's dream: Stolen life, second chance. People.* Retrieved from people.com/archive/a-wronged-mans-dream-stolen-life-second-chance-vol-78-no-8/.

Brown, K W, Creswell, J D, & Ryan, R M (Eds). (2015) *Handbook of mindfulness: Theory, research, and practice.* New York, NY, US: Guilford Press.

Daugherty, P. (2014) *Facing death, Lauren Hill teaches us life lessons. Cincinnati Inquirer,* A1, A6, A7.

Dalio, R. (2017) *Principles.* New York, US: Simon & Schuster.

Eastwood, C (director). (2009) *Invictus.* Liberty Pictures, Warner Brothers.

Finerman, W, Newirth, C, Starkey, S, Tisch, S (Producers), & Zemeckis, R (Director). (1994) *Forrest Gump* [Motion Picture]. United States: Paramount Pictures.

Frankl, V E. (1992) *Man's search for meaning: An introduction to logotherapy* (4th ed.) (I Lasch, Trans.). Boston, MA, US: Beacon Press.

Germer, C K. (2009) *The mindful path to self-compassion: Freeing yourself from destructive thoughts and emotions.* New York, NY, US: Guilford Press.

Gottman, J M & Silver, N. (1999) *The seven principles for making marriage work.* New York: Three Rivers Press.

Hackford, T (Director). (2004) *Ray.* Universal Pictures.

Hawking, S. (2017) *A brief history of time.* Bantum Books.

Helgeland, B. (2013) *42.* Legendary Pictures, Warner Brothers.

Henley, W E. (1875) *Invictus.* Book of verses. New York: Scribner and Welford.

Howard, R. (1995). *Apollo 13.* Universal Pictures, Imagine Entertainment.

Isaacson, W. (2015) *Steve Jobs.* New York, NY, US: Simon & Schuster Paperbacks.

Kabat-Zinn, J. (2005) *Full catastrophe living: Using the wisdom of your body and mind to face stress, pain, and illness.* (15th anniversary ed.). New York, NY, US: Delta Trade Paperback/Bantam Dell.

Linehan, M M. (2015) *DBT skills training: Handouts and worksheets.* New York: Guilford.

Lovell, J & Kluger, J. (1994) *Lost Moon: The perilous voyage of Apollo 13.* Houghton Mifflin Company.

Mangold, J (director). (2005) *Walk the Line.* 20th Century Fox. Rinehart & Winston.

Passons, W R. (1975). *Gestalt approaches in counseling.* New York, Holt.

Robinson, J. (1995) *I never had it made: An autobiography.* New York, HarperCollins.

Roemer, L & Orsillo, S M. (2009) *Guides to evidence-based treatment. Mindfulness- and acceptance-based behavioral therapies in practice.* New York, NY, US: Guilford Press.

Shimizu, E H (Producer) & Belic, R (Director). (2011) *Happy* [Motion Picture]. United States: Wadi Rum Films, Inc.

Dialectics

Chapter 7

WHAT MARSHA LINEHAN SAYS ABOUT DIALECTICS IN DBT

A major goal of Dialectical Behavior Therapy is to help the client begin to think in more dialectical terms, but this is not an easy task. Discussing dialectics, Linehan states "it can be difficult to grasp" (1993, p. 121). Linehan explains "reality is not static, but is comprised by internal opposing forces" ("thesis" and "antithesis") out of whose integration ("synthesis") evolves a new set of opposing forces (p. 32). These opposites are called polarities. In one metaphor, Linehan compares her work with a patient as if they are on a teeter-totter, at the extremes, but working to get to the middle, where they can create a synthesis. She points out this combination of opposites (or polarities) is true in physics, with an atom being made out of positive and negative particles, and even the smallest particle of matter is balanced by anti-matter:

Dialectical thinking requires the ability to transcend the polarities and to see reality as complex and multifaceted; to entertain contradictory thoughts and points of view, and to unite and integrate them ... [persons needing DBT] think in extremes and hold rigidly to points of view. Life is black or white, viewed in dichotomous terms ... The overall goal of DBT is not to get patients to view reality as a series of grays, but rather to help them see both black and white, to achieve a synthesis of the two that does not negate the reality of the other.

(1993, p. 121)

Dr Linehan points out that there are various polarities to consider. One example (see p. 74) is when a person has problems with emotion regulation, with relationships, or with a self-destructive behavior, is it the person's fault and thus responsibility to change, or is it due to a dysfunctional or unsupportive environment? Is it the individual's responsibility to change, or is it their social group/society's responsibility to improve the situation? The dialectical answer is both: there needs to be a synthesis of individual and societal responsibility and effort. This question is one in which our society is deeply polarized, thinking it is either the individual's responsibility or the responsibility of society to do the work of change. Either of these points of view are wildly oversimplified, but make for sensational talk radio.

Another polarity that Dr Linehan highlights is the struggle between acceptance and change. The therapist must accept that the patient is doing the best he or she can, but also insist that they try harder, in order to produce behavioral change.

When thinking of this polarity of change and acceptance, I remember a young man who I worked with who experienced extreme mood swings. He would escalate to perhaps 95 on the SUDS scale, and verbally lash out at his parents or me. He would call or text me, calling me a charlatan, saying I didn't care for him, that I was only in it for the money, etc. I responded with acceptance, and he eventually would calm down, but then go through another rage cycle days later. One time he stormed out of our DBT skills group, but was making so much noise in the street that I had to leave the group to my co-leader and try to quiet him down. He knew I had recently bought a fairly new but certified pre-owned 2016 Dodge Charger SXT, the first "fancy" car I have ever owned. He threatened to throw a brick though the windshield. I calmly said, "If you damage my Charger, you can no longer be my patient." After this statement, the rage cycles dropped dramatically. He needed acceptance, but he also needed a push to change, and a limitation to acceptance. I think we found the middle path.

Another polarity is between changing one's emotional response versus accepting the painful emotion, rather than avoiding it. A third polarity includes seeing our problem behaviors as both maladaptive and adaptive. If the problem behavior did not have some adaptive value for our functioning, we would not be doing it, yet the behavior is also maladaptive and making the overall trajectory of our life worse. Still a fourth example of a dialectical point of view is that all truth does not come through "logical reasoning and intellectual analysis," (Linehan, 1993, p. 204) but through personal experience, including emotional experience.

Learning to see the world from a dialectical point of view is not a quick or easy task, but I hope the following metaphors and stories will help you begin to grasp the "D" in DBT.

UNDERSTANDING DIALECTICS—START WITH SIMILAR WORDS YOU *DO* UNDERSTAND

When helping persons to understand "the D in DBT," I suggest looking to similar words one already understands.

Think of the word "dialogue." A dialogue is a discussion between two persons in which information freely flows between both parties. Both are talking and listening. This is in contrast to a monologue, where one person is doing all the talking, and does not invite the other party to share or express their reactions. Perhaps the former person even forbids the other person to express their thoughts. The monologuing person monopolizes the discussion. Both sides do not get to express themselves. One or both sides are not listening, at least one side is not heard. Maybe this is what singer-songwriter Paul Simon was talking about in "The Sound of Silence" (1964) when he spoke of people listening without hearing.

I have observed in my 25 years as a clinical psychologist (and my 62 years as a human) that when people have problems in relationships, it is often because the relationship has descended into being a functional monologue. Yes, both sides are talking, but one or both are not listening, and so there is not a true exchange of thought and emotion. Recall the Interpersonal Effectiveness module: practicing both the Objective Effectiveness (DEAR MAN) and Relationship Effectiveness (GIVE) skills assures us that both sides are heard.

Using DEAR MAN skills makes sure you are speaking your truth effectively, and the GIVE skills make sure you listen and validate the other person's idea(s). Using these skills makes the discussion a *dialogue*, a discussion that is truly dialectical.

Marsha Linehan explains the meaning of dialectical: "There is always more than one side to anything that exists; look for both sides [and] ask 'where is the kernel of truth on the other side?' Find truth in both sides" (Linehan, 2015b, p. 290). This is true, even with parts of ourselves.

A second word that is similar to dialectical is "dialect." A dialect is a common language, shared by a group, that allows intimate communication. As such, a dialect is a bridge between all parties that use it to reach common understanding. This is exactly what dialectical perception and thinking does: it builds the bridge between different, even opposite ways of looking at things to find a higher truth that more closely approximates reality.

UNDERSTANDING DIALECTICS—WINNING AND LOSING

Understanding what Marsha Linehan means when she talks about a dialectical approach to life can be challenging at first. The idea that two things are opposite, contradictory, and yet both true seems absurd. However, the more I have thought about dialectics, the more I appreciate dialectic wisdom. Dialectics inform not just psychology but the physical sciences as well. Dr Linehan points out (1993, p. 32; 2015b, p. 286) that this combination of opposites (or polarities) is true in physics, with an atom being made out of positive and negative particles, and even the smallest particle of matter is balanced by anti-matter.

Here is an example of dialectics that comes from my experience as a parent. Both of my sons are very competitive. My oldest son, Noah, emerged as a very good athlete by the time he turned six years old. Noah really wanted to win at every sport he competed in.

Winning and losing are opposites. So are the attitudes of "I want to win" and "it is okay to lose." One time, Noah's soccer team was in a tournament and he scored a goal that put his team ahead one to nothing. The coaches, who valued each child equally, pulled Noah out for a substitution to allow another player to have as much playing time. During a pretty big chunk of time that Noah sat on the bench, the other team pulled ahead by the score of two to one. When Noah was put back into the game, he was so emotionally rattled by the fact that his team was now losing that he could not play his best game. He was visibly upset, on the verge of tears and was not able to play with the confidence that he normally did.

At this point, I began to think about how the desire to win is best *counterbalanced* with the attitude of it is okay to lose. When we Radically Accept that sometimes we *will* lose, and yet the game is still worth playing, it frees us up to play with our highest degree of motivation *and* we are freed from the debilitating effects of the fear of losing. This is a dialectical approach to winning and losing.

It is good to win and it is okay, even good, to lose. Both are true.

DIALECTICS—UNDERSTANDING POLARITIES

Understanding dialectics is not an easy task. Though I am certainly not a physicist, an example from science is the conundrum of understanding the properties of light. In some ways, light behaves like a particle; in other ways, it behaves like a wave. As such, light defies our conventional understanding of the laws of nature, but this points to how reality is often more complex than our usual way of thinking.

One of the dialectical contradictions that Marsha Linehan discusses is the polarity of Acceptance and Change (Linehan, 1993). She challenges DBT therapists to accept that clients are doing the very best that they can, *and* at the same time, they need to do better. People with deep emotional problems such as depression, anxiety, and self-destructive behaviors are doing the very best they can, *and* they need to do better and change their behavior. That's contradictory, but it's also true.

Psychologist Sidney J Blatt, PhD points out another dialectical contradiction. All of us need to establish personally satisfying relationships, be part of a group, and abide by the rules of the group (Blatt, 2008). At the same time, we need a sense of individual self, one that is not eclipsed by the culture of our group. This is the dialectic of individuality versus relatedness. These two dynamics clash, they contradict, but they also need each other. No one can develop a good sense of themselves as an individual without a supportive and loving group of other humans to nurture their individuality. And yet, to have a positive relationship with a group of people, one needs a strong sense of individuality. If you don't believe me, think of someone who conforms to everything that others say. Initially they may be welcomed into the group, but later the group resents their presence because they have no personality of their own. People who agree to everything their group says are extremely boring people.

I experienced this conflict as a college freshman. I went to a very conservative religious school where the main objective was to prepare young men for the ministry. Once a year, both the men's and women's dormitories had an open house; this was the only time we were ever allowed to go into the dorm of the opposite sex. After cleaning my room, I came up with the grand idea of flashing some of my individuality. I decided to put on display, on my side of the dorm room, my collection of vintage Johnny Cash albums. There they were: Cash's two famous albums recorded inside of prisons (Folsom Prison and San Quentin), albums about blue collar workers, the old West, albums from his rockabilly days in the 1950s, the Ring of Fire album, even an album about the Holy Land.

The president of the college toured both dorms. When he got to my room he entered with a friendly smile, but this quickly turned into a look of astonishment, disapproval, perhaps with a bit of disgust thrown into the mix (at least, that's what I perceived). He didn't say much with words, but the look on his face communicated the fact that this sort of preoccupation was a waste of my focus when it came to becoming a good preacher. All of a sudden, I felt ashamed of my collection, and how I deviated from my classmates. The truth was, I didn't have a strong enough sense of myself as a good and solid person to continue to assert my individuality. I gave away some of my individuality (but, thank God, not the albums), to fit in. I gave into one side of the polarity to fit in, but denied the other side (myself). Not surprisingly, I became a very dull (and soon, depressed) preacher, primarily because I wasn't being myself.

Psychologist Thomas Marra lists many of the polarities that humans need to grapple with and balance (Marra, 2005). For example, stability versus flexibility. Most of us need a fairly stable schedule/routine to function with any degree of effectiveness. At the same time, we need to be able to approach life in a flexible manner that allows us to organize our behavior and schedule to meet the needs and demands facing us. Another polarity is cultivating our skills and capabilities versus accepting our limitations. As a 62-year-old man with average athletic ability, I have come to accept that no matter how fully I devote myself to skill development, I will never play basketball in the NBA.

THESIS, ANTITHESIS, AND SYNTHESIS—COME TAKE A TRIP ON THE GLORY ROAD

Dialectics emerged from several sources, a primary one being philosopher Georg Wilhelm Friedrich Hegel. Hegel wrote about "thesis"—an idea or paradigm. However, at some point, "antithesis" emerges, the exact opposite of thesis, contradicting it. People come up with the antithesis because, though thesis works some of the time, in other cases it does not, leading to the development of an antithesis, an opposite theory. However, thesis did hold considerable truth, and so there is great tension between thesis and antithesis. This great tension leads to an eventual integration of these two opposites, which is a synthesis of both.

Thomas Lynch gives a real-world example of thesis-antithesis-synthesis:

Dialectical thinking involves three developmental stages: a thesis (such as "self-control is always necessary"), giving rise to antithesis ("too much self-control is always unhealthy"), which contradicts and seems to negate the thesis, while the tension between the two opposite perspectives is resolved via a synthesis of the two opposite perspectives that ideally results in higher order functioning, not simply a compromise.

(Lynch, 2018b, p. 18)

This thesis-antithesis-synthesis process is beautifully portrayed in the film *Glory Road* (Gartner, 2006), a true story based on the biography of the same name by Don Haskins. Haskins was recruited in 1961 to become the basketball coach at Texas Western University (now the University of Texas at El Paso). Texas Western was a Division 1 school, but had limited resources and was not a prestigious program. By the mid-1960s, Haskins began to do the unthinkable for a school in the south: recruit a large number of African American players.

The film depicts the players Haskins recruits as all well-schooled in a flashy style of play that emphasizes well-executed fakes, dribbling behind the back, and dunking the basketball, the latter being in part to establish a sense of dominance over their opponent (the thesis). Haskins labels this flashy style of play as based in insecurity and compels his team to play discipline basketball, devoted to the fundamentals including defense, rebounding and none of the show-boating that the former style featured. Haskin's style constituted the antithesis.

In the film, Texas Western becomes a winning program, even moving up in the national rankings, but they run into a juggernaut when they play the #4 team in the nation, the University of Iowa Hawkeyes. Texas Western is down 46-30 at the half. In the locker room, Haskins is chastising the team for getting beat so badly, resuming his lecture on defense, "fundamental basketball", etc. Point guard Bobby Joe Hill speaks up, and says Texas Western cannot beat Iowa playing the coach's game and pleads that the coach lets them play their game. Coach Haskins is at a crucial decision point. He ponders what Bobby Joe has said, then replies, "OK, we play your game ... *and* we play my game, too."

Texas Western comes out and runs their offense in the style of the majority of players, the flashy African American style that utilizes deceptive moves like dribbling behind the back (thesis). They begin to score at ease versus Iowa. But they are also playing the fundamental, defense-oriented style of Haskins (antithesis). A synthesis has occurred. Texas Western comes back to beat Iowa. Later, Texas Western stuns the world by winning the 1966 NCAA Championship. To quote Thomas Lynch (see above citation), "higher-order functioning" was the result, "not simply a compromise."

Years later, in his 2006 autobiography (Haskins & Wetzel, 2006), Coach Haskins did acknowledge that initially he thought Bobbly Joe Hill was "a hot dog" (p. 126). Over time, Haskins began to realize that he was "overcoaching" Bobby Joe by trying to micromanage his playing style. Haskins spoke of the polarized positions of he and Bobby Joe, saying "Bobby Joe was just stubborn ... I guess he was a little like his coach" (p. 130). Fortunately for Texas Western, these two found the middle path.

Your DBT skills trainers and DBT therapist will demonstrate new ways of thinking and behaving that will seem foreign to you, even unnatural. This is the "D" in DBT.

Moving from non-dialectical thinking to dialectical thinking is often awkward at minimum, and scary is frequently the norm. But this is often the missing link in building a life worth living.

DIALECTICS—TRUST BUT VERIFY

Trust versus suspicion is another dialectical dimension or polarity in which both sides must be embraced to build a life worth living, one which Dr Linehan points out in the *DBT Skills Training Handouts and Worksheets* (Linehan, 2015a, p. 153). If a person is entirely trusting, dishonest and predatory people will take advantage of them. These persons are gullible and naïve. However, if a person is suspicious to a high degree, they trust no one, build no beneficial alliances, and live in constant fear, vigilance, and loneliness. We describe these people as paranoid.

To build a life worth living, we must simultaneously be trusting and vigilant, taking people at their word while looking out for red flags indicating something is wrong. We need to have one foot in trust, the other in suspicion.

This attitude is illustrated by world leaders who want to reduce the number of nuclear weapons on planet Earth, who take the attitude of "trust, but verify."

DIALECTICS IN ACTION: PLAYFUL IRREVERENCE VERSUS COMPASSIONATE GRAVITY

Psychologist Thomas Lynch has adapted DBT, which was developed by Marsha Linehan to help persons with problems with under-control of their behavior, to help persons with problematic over-control. These uptight, super-serious, and compulsive persons frequently suffer from depression and have minimal, if any, close relationships. Lynch calls his adaptation Radically Open Dialectical Behavior Therapy (or RO DBT).

One of the polarities Lynch writes about is what he calls "playful irreverence versus compassionate gravity." Linehan also recommends therapists to have an irreverent sense of humor, and in the Interpersonal Effectiveness module she recommends using an "Easy Manner," which includes lightness and humor as part of Relationship Effectiveness.

Note that "playful irreverence" and "compassionate gravity" are opposites. Lynch is directing us to do both at the same time. An illustration of this is found in the film *Walk the Line*. Johnny Cash is playing a raucous concert inside California's notorious Folsom Prison. During a brief break offstage, the warden asks him not to play anymore songs "that remind the men they are in prison." Cash smirks and replies, "Do you think they forgot?"

We can be compassionate and serious for someone else (or our self), and at the same time be playful and irreverent. Irreverent means we don't take anyone too seriously, and we point out their inconsistences, shortcomings, and violations of social norms. But we do so with compassion, not a mean-spirited or judgmental attitude.

Through the decades, I have found myself being extraordinarily silly with some, but not all of my psychotherapy clients. For the first couple of decades, I wondered why I did this with some, but not all. I wondered if I was letting my professionalism slip. But I always noticed these clients were engaging in significant cognitive, emotional, and behavioral change. They were getting better. When I revisited what Marsha Linehan wrote in 1993 about irreverent humor, I realized that I was acting on intuition (not pure logic or a therapy manual). Later, I read what Lynch said in his therapy manual: "In RO DBT, Silliness is No Laughing Matter" (Lynch, 2018a, p. 4). When my clients were too pensive, brooding, and serious, I modeled the opposite to try to strike a dialectical balance.

Finding the synthesis between playful irreverence and compassionate gravity is important. It is not just joking one minute, then being ultra-serious and somber the next. Playful irreverence should poke fun at the irony of a situation or perhaps at a behavioral transgression of a person, but it should never be judgmental of the person. I often poke fun at myself, but never in a meanspirited or judgmental way. Playful irreverence should be coupled with empathy and respect. If my patients ever felt I was disrespecting them, I would have, at minimum, lost them as clients.

When a person is exclusively playful and silly, they are probably using it to avoid the gravity of the issues in their life. When a person treats everything as one big joke, their lives tend to be superficial, and they experience little forward movement as they move through their lifespan. When persons are exclusively caring, compassionate, somber, and marked with pronounced gravity, others intuitively avoid them and reject their input. Other people perceive them to be super-serious to the point of being polarizing, inflexibly approaching life in a way that is, at minimum not very fun, and in most cases unhealthy. Think of the teachers, ministers, priests, and youth leaders who were always ultra-serious. Did you want to be like them?

Think of the persons who have had significant influence in your life. My guess is they walked the middle path between playful irreverence and compassionate gravity, doing some of both. They probably never heard of the word "dialectical." But they knew how to live it.

ANOTHER POLARITY TO DIALECTICALLY SYNTHESIZE: SELF-CRITICISM VERSUS SELF-ACCEPTANCE

Dennis Tirch, Laura Silberstein, and Russell Kolts (2016) point out how one of Buddhism's main teachings is the importance of walking "the middle path" between extremes. One of these polarities concerns self-criticism versus self-compassion.

Most of us struggle with self-criticism. When we do something incorrectly (or avoid it altogether), we engage in self-punishment, berating ourselves with self-talk that focuses on telling ourselves how bad we are. What we don't realize is this type of self-criticism functions primarily to create psychological pain: we think punishing ourselves will create positive behavioral change. Scientific research points out that punishment is of limited value. It can stop a problem behavior, but at the same time it tends to also elicit oppositional sentiment, perhaps even rebellion. One of the problems with this approach is our psyche is sending most of its resources to punish and humiliate ourselves, with few resources left to motivate positive behavior change. Punishment cannot motivate us to engage in an effective behavior. It can only (sometimes) stop a negative behavior.

If harsh self-criticism has helped you achieve the behavior you want, more power to you. In most cases, it bogs us down. We are better served by dialectically integrating critique of our behavior with self-compassion and self-acceptance. Tirch, Silberstein, and Kolts point out that being critical of our behavior is helpful, if it is not judgment (p. 52). Doing this results in self-criticism being "compassionate correction" of our behavior rather than "shameful attacking" of our self.

Think of the two alternatives to this dialectical approach. One would be to endorse one side of the polarity, harsh self-criticism by endlessly berating and humiliating yourself. Every time you make a mistake, you tell yourself you are a piece of shit. The other side of the polarity is equally problematic. If we accept ourselves, no matter what, we will never change. We never break bad habits, push ourselves to get better or learn anything that requires effort. If I would have allowed myself to live at this end of the polarity, I would still be playing the same three guitar chords for the last 48 years, and so I am glad that I don't accept my level of guitar playing unconditionally.

Marsha Linehan points to the need to balance this polarity between working to improve our self and accepting our self just as we are. Remember that one of Marsha's primary influences was studying and practicing Zen Buddhism (while also being a practicing Roman Catholic). Thinking and living dialectically requires us to find "the middle path."

DIALECTICAL FAILURE—TONY CLIFTON

Man on the Moon (Forman, 1999) is a film about the life and death of comedian Andy Kaufman. Kaufman was an unconventional but supremely talented comedian who was enthralled with keeping his audience off balance. He often created scenarios and scenes which confused the audience as to whether he was joking or serious about a subject.

One such scenario was about a character created by Andy and creative partner Bob Zumda, a lounge singer by the name of Tony Clifton. Kaufman insisted that Tony Clifton be part of his concert show, as well as have airtime during TV appearances. Often Andy played the part of Clifton, wearing an elaborate disguise which hid his identity, other times it was Zumda. Tony Clifton was deliberately rude and abrasive to his audience. He would insult them, with some in the audience finding this funny, and others being offended, but most were confused, not knowing if Clifton was intending to be funny or if he was deliberately insulting them. At times, when audiences where convinced it was Kaufman playing the role of Tony Clifton, Andy would emerge from backstage to congratulate the crude and arrogant lounge singer (who on these occasions was being played by Bob Zumda).

As Kaufman's career moved forward, the negativity that he sowed with characters like Tony Clifton, as well as his professional wrestling villain persona (who continually insulted wrestling fans) took a toll on his career and he became increasingly unpopular. The film *Man on the Moon* depicts Andy as thrilled that he could deceive and enrage his audience to such an extraordinary degree. People were so upset with him that *Saturday Night Live* held an election, giving viewers a chance to vote on whether Andy should stay on the show—the majority of Americans voted him off. His manager, George Shapiro, confronted him, pointing out that Andy had lost perspective on what showbiz is about. Shapiro noted that Andy was highly amused by his ability to dupe and insult the audience, achieving his goal and perceiving this as success. Shapiro confronted him, noting that Andy needed to entertain his audience, to make them laugh, and make them happy.

In a sense, Andy Kaufman (at least as depicted in the film) failed at the dialectic of any medium of art. Art is not about the artist making themselves happy. Nor is art about making the audience happy. Good art, whether it is a painting, sculpture, music, theater, or comedy, has the effect of making *both* the artist and the audience happy.

Pleasing our self is very different from pleasing the other person. Yet relationships only work when live in a dialectical manner, pleasing both our self and others. Is art about the artist or the audience? The dialectical answer is "yes."

UNDERSTANDING DIALECTICS—DEPENDENCE AND INDEPENDENCE

One of the areas that many people struggle with is dealing with the concepts of dependence and independence. When persons do not dialectically integrate these two poles, problems ensue.

Many people think of dependence as "bad" and independence as "good," but this very non-dialectical view of human existence, and invariably leads to dissatisfaction and interpersonal failure. Dependence and independence are opposites, but if you are beginning to grasp dialectics, it may not surprise you that they are both true and "good."

When we define a person as dependent, we mean they think of themselves as incapable of doing much of anything on their own. They refrain from increasing their skills, fearing doing so will jeopardize their connection to the persons they depend on. Most of us do not want to be dependent to this degree because we understand this leaves us vulnerable to the whims of the person or persons we are depending on, and thus vulnerable to be forced into things we may not want to do. However, if our fear of being abandoned eclipses our desire for mastery and independence, we sacrifice the latter to preserve the former.

Many of us think of independence as "good"—the more independent we are, the better. Who wouldn't want to be more capable of accomplishing things on our own? However, this is where we can also run into problems. I have worked with a number of persons who are enamored with being "independent," with not needing to rely on someone else, and this leads to unforeseen consequences. The fanatically independent person may love to help others, but is extremely averse to being helped by someone else. This hyper-independent person refuses help from others, often when they very much need it. They hide their problems until their health, financial, or interpersonal problem has compounded to the point that the problems may not be reversible. The "independence junky" feels guilty and perhaps even ashamed to receive help from others, yet they expect others to take their help with no guilt feelings whatsoever. Others feel uncomfortable with this sort of one-way relationship. An independence junky may tell their children "there is no shame in receiving help," but they model the exact opposite, acting as if receiving help is shameful. Which message do think is going to be more persuasive for the child? Think of this: if everyone was "the independent one," who would there be to accept the help they offer?

A common tradition in most wedding receptions is for the bride and groom to cut the cake together, then intertwine their arms and feed each other a piece of cake. Often they turn this into a big joke, smashing it in each other's face. As a psychologist who does a lot of couples therapy, I often cite this tradition, and ask the couple if they know what this symbolizes. Sadly, I have had only one couple know the answer (which may be part of why many of these couples need therapy). I explain this ritual is a metaphor for a healthy marriage: it is all about taking care of one another's needs, in effect, feeding them. Smashing the cake deflects people from understanding the profound symbolism.

Gestalt Therapy is a school of therapy that has much in common with DBT (Linehan, 1993, p. 22). Gestalt Therapy emphasizes the person in relationship to their environment (Mann, 2010). If you think of it, this is our entire existence: we are embedded in our environment, and our every behavior is an effort in extracting resources from our environment. I challenge you to find an exception to this point of view. The resources we require include not only air, water, and food, but psychological needs as well. We are entirely dependent on our environment. As such, there is no such thing as "independence"—without our environment, including our social environment, we would die.

What do we commonly mean when we use the terms dependent and independent? A dependent person tries to get their needs met by being passive, like a baby bird that expects the mama to bring the worm to them. The independent person is the bird who puts forth effort to fly on their own and gather their own worms.

But once again, consider this: the "independent" bird is entirely dependent on the environment for producing worms. Both the skill and effort of the bird (independence) and the environment (something entirely out of the bird's control) must be there … or the bird starves and dies.

Much of our psychological needs are for interaction with other people. None of us are truly independent. But what if we become passive and expect others to take care of us? If we become this dependent, all but the most unhealthy of people will run from us.

So, do you want to be a dependent or independent person? The Wise Mind, dialectical answer is … both!

DIALECTICAL DILEMMA: WORDS HURT VERSUS "STICKS AND STONES MAY BREAK MY BONES, BUT YOUR WORDS WILL NEVER HURT ME"

Here is a dialectical dilemma, two ideas that contradict each other, both of which are true.

Words can harm others. Marsha Linehan documents this clearly, pointing to the damaging effect of invalidation. Researcher John Briere (1992) points to the fact that not only does verbal abuse harm children, but that it is likely as psychologically harmful as other forms of abuse.

I am fascinated how the teachings of Jesus take this point of view. In the Sermon on the Mount, Jesus said "You have heard that it was said … do not murder … but I tell you, anyone who says to his brother "Raca" [an Aramaic term of contempt] is answerable to the judgment." Likewise, Jesus said anyone who calls someone a "fool" (a pretty invalidating label) is likewise in danger of God's judgment (Matthew 5:21, 22, paraphrased from the New International Version).

Here is the other side of the polarity: the adage "sticks and stones can break my bones, but your words will never hurt me." This is a useful way of looking at things. If we take on this mindset, we can build resilience to the insults and putdowns of others.

A dialectical point of view enables us to integrate these two contradictory truths.

DIALECTICS AND THE BIBLE

A well-known passage from the Bible goes as follows:

> There is a time for everything, and a season for every activity under heaven
> A time to be born, and a time to die
> A time to plant, and a time to uproot

A time to kill, and a time to heal

A time to tear down, and a time to build

A time to weep, and a time to laugh

A time to mourn, and a time to dance

A time to scatter stones, and a time to gather stones together

A time to embrace, and a time to refrain

A time to search, and a time to give up

A time to keep, and a time to throw away

A time to tear, and a time to mend

A time to be silent, and a time to speak

A time to love, and a time to hate

A time for war, and a time for peace

> This ancient wisdom is found in the book of Ecclesiastes, chapter 3 versus 1–8.

This passage reminds us of the trouble people get into when they try to live in a non-dialectical manner. Think of a hoarder: here is a person who believes it is always time to keep, and never time to throw away. Some people are serious all the time (weeping), whereas others react to everything in life as if it is one big joke. The former is frequently depressed and joyless, the latter gets stuck in unproductive patterns of living because they fail to see the serious issues that need attention. A person who is stuck in a relationship with an abusive partner may be held back because they do not permit hate to emerge, hate is the rocket fuel to break free of the gravity of that destructive relationship. However, there will be a time to let go of hate, because if hate is held onto it will keep the memory of the abusive ex-partner on the main stage of that person's consciousness and will poison their soul.

Psychologist Thomas Marra reminds DBT therapists that "no specific 'end' of the dialectic is always appropriate or reasonable, but that 'place' along the dialectic continuum is determined by contextual variables and the goals and objectives of the person" (p. 116). Our contextual variables determine whether it is "a time to mourn, or a time to dance."

Another psychologist and author, Jordan Peterson (1999), points out that life is made up of opposites, such as dealing with the known versus the unknown, order versus chaos. We all need some order, otherwise we would be reinventing the wheel in every situation we encounter. Thank goodness I go home to the same wife, family, and house every night. I need some things to stay the same.

But a life of all predictability and order becomes a life of monotony, yielding no innovation or growth. Some chaos, some unpredictable events and forces need to shake up our orderly world, or there would be no novelty, no invention, no growth. Our lives would be tediously predictable (like in the film, *Groundhog's Day*). The old saying goes, "Necessity is the mother of invention." No chaos, no necessity, means no invention. Stagnation and boredom rule.

When something unpredictable happens, do not fall into the trap of saying it is "bad" (which would be a judgment). It may be unpleasant, it may be difficult. It probably will thrust you into the world of the unknown, unchartered waters, which of course will force you to swim in ways you have never done previously. But this is not "bad."

Here is a real life story that illustrates this. When he was five years old, Johnny Cash was growing up on a small farm in Arkansas. The year was 1937, and in the spring, severe rainstorms produced the biggest flood in history of the Mississippi River. The levy at Wilson, Arkansas broke, and when the flood waters reached the Cash family farm, they had to flee to higher ground. The flood waters reached the house, sweeping through their home, destroying many of their possessions, washing all their crops away, and eliminating their principle income for that year (Cash, 1997, p. 20). Sound like a bad thing?

Cash wrote one of his best songs, "Five Feet High and Rising," about the flood. He would frequently introduce the song in concert by describing how the flood deposited a great deal of rich black topsoil on their land. Though the flood filled their house with mud, it also led to more bountiful crops, and the Cashes made a lot more money. One of Johnny's fondest memories is how his father turned their front door into a makeshift boat to sail him and his younger siblings to safety. And when he was an adult, he wrote "Five Feet High and Rising."

Dr Linehan states:

> The goal of dialectics is not to get the participants to see reality as a series of grays, but rather to help them see both black and white, and to achieve a synthesis of the two that does not negate the reality of the other.
>
> (Linehan, 2015b, p. 291)

The flood of 1937 was for the Cashes both good and bad. Bad that they lost their crops that year, bad that many possessions were damaged or lost. The flood was good for their improved topsoil and improvement in agricultural output for the next several years. Good that it was the catalyst for a great song.

There is a time and a season for everything. Even floods and dry weather. The writer of the book of Ecclesiastes understood this thousands of years ago. The world is a dialectical place.

MY FAVORITE DIALECTICAL SONG: "SAVE SOME TIME TO DREAM" BY JOHN MELLENCAMP

The best way to enjoy this metaphor is to go to YouTube, look up the song, and play the live version of Mellencamp singing it on Late Night with David Letterman. You will not only hear, but see what I am talking about in this metaphor.

The song "Save Some Time to Dream" was released by John Mellencamp in 2010 on his album, *No Better than This* (2010). Shortly thereafter, he appeared on Letterman, singing this song accompanied only by his acoustic guitar, plugged into a single amplifier. With no band behind him, the spotlight shines solely on the lyrics, which I find both profound and very dialectical.

The first verse admonishes the listener to save time to dream, as well as for one's self, and the second verse urges us to preserve a good chunk of our time for those we love, as well as for our own creativity, because at the end of our lives, we will realize these should have been our highest priorities.

The chorus then challenges the listener to think about an existential issue. Could it be that there is no afterlife? If this is possible, why do we act as if the here-and-now is just a warm up for something later? Pondering this possibility sets us up for a dialectical struggle. Most Americans, Canadians, and Europeans believe in God or some sort of divine spirit, which in turn also includes a belief in an afterlife. For those of us who do, Mellencamp's chorus, which suggests that this life is all there is, is a stark antithesis. Some folks are afraid to even entertain this question, but many people I know who would identify themselves as "believers" have also looked at the other possibility (the antithesis), something inherent in the thesis. Even one of the Biblical writers struggled with whether this life could it be all there is:

> Man's fate is like that of the animals, the same fate awaits them both, as one dies, so does the other. All have the same breath, man has no advantage over the animal … All go to the same place, and all return to the dust, and to dust all will return. Who knows if the spirit of man rises upward and the spirit of the animal goes down into the earth?
>
> Ecclesiastes 3:19–21, New International Version

The Bible is not really "a book," but a collection of books. My understanding of the Bible is that it is more dialectical (containing opposing viewpoints amongst its various books) than most people realize. But that is the topic for another book.

The next verse deals with another dialectic: Mellencamp points out that sorrow and failure will come our way, and rather than this being "bad," sorrow and failure are two factors that actually enrich our lives, preparing us to be more successful at living a meaningful life. Many people view failure in non-dialectical terms, as "bad." Failure can be one of our most important teachers, and as Mellencamp said, it can give us strength in the long run. I think I have learned more from my failures than my successes.

The fourth verse implores us to keep our mind open, especially when it comes to our own mistakes, and to question our faith. Skepticism is the opposite of faith, and this verse embraces skepticism. In dialectical terms, skepticism is the antithesis, and faith is the thesis. But in true dialectical fashion, Mellencamp's skepticism does not banish faith, rather it complements faith, as seen in the fifth and final verse. Here Mellencamp directs us to turn back and embrace our faith along with our skepticism. This final verse also points to another dialectic, between our religious beliefs and our actions. He implores us to deal with those who don't understand us with loving kindness, something that DBT and mindfulness approaches in general identify as a core factor of living a mindful life.

I wanted to include the actual lyrics of this song in their entirety in this book, but unfortunately, I did not receive permission from the publisher of the song in time for their inclusion for publication. Take my word for it, the words are beautiful and profound.

If you haven't yet watched Mellencamp sing this on the Letterman show via YouTube, I invite you to do it now. Notice as Mellencamp sings the lyrics that question the existence of an afterlife (and perhaps even God), there is a very conspicuous statue of Jesus, standing on top of Mellencamp's Fender amplifier. Notice how Jesus is holding his hands (the "Willing Hands" position found in the Distress Tolerance module). Jesus is holding his hands in an open position, suggesting a reaching out, perhaps even acceptance.

Faith and skepticism. Thesis and antithesis. Maybe this four-minute clip of Mellencamp on the Letterman show demonstrates his ultimate synthesis.

LIVING DIALECTICALLY—DON'T LIMIT YOURSELF TO PEOPLE WHO AGREE WITH YOU

One of the most self-limiting things any person can do is to limit your contact to only people who think like you. This is the psychological equivalent of inbreeding, of marrying your cousin. Talking and listening to only persons who agree with you will impoverish your intellect, and your spirit as well.

When we are living dialectically, we open ourselves to the contradictions and oversights of our point of view. We welcome critique, seeing it as a gift, rather than as our enemy.

I admire great intellects, such as the creator of DBT, Marsha Linehan. What did Linehan, the behavior therapist, do before publishing her 1993 book that launched DBT? She spent a significant amount of time talking about her approach with experts from very different therapy approaches. Linehan sought out the input from two prominent psychoanalytic leaders, Otto Kernberg and John Clarkin. She also had a longtime friend, Sally Parks, a Jungian analysist, with whom she debated behavioral versus Jungian approaches to therapy. Marsha was not trying to defeat these persons in the "debate." Marsha was more interested in the exchange of ideas, in their critique, assuming this dialogue, this back and forth, would actually move her closer to the truth as each party critiqued the other. Marsha's thoughts were the thesis, the psychodynamic experts were the antithesis (opposite, contradictory, but "true"). Without the antithesis of the psychodynamic experts, Marsha's therapy, DBT, would have never achieved a state of synthesis.

A verse in the Bible I have always been intrigued with says, "for the time will come when men ... to suit their own desire, will gather around them a great number of teachers to say what their itching ears want to hear" (II Timothy 4:3). Surrounding ourselves with persons who tell us only what we want to hear is an easy path, but not a dialectical one.

To live dialectically is to listen to all points of view, not just the ones you like or want to believe. It takes humility to embrace a dialectical approach to life, to admit that you are not omnipotent, that you might be mistaken or only see one part of the puzzle. It takes courage to open one's self up the dialogue between thesis and antithesis that leads to meaningful behavior change. But staying stuck in same old view of reality will keep one stuck in the same dissatisfying life.

UNDERSTANDING DIALECTICS—JOE MORGAN

In the DBT Skills Training Manual for DBT group leaders, Marsha Linehan discusses how the dialectical worldview permeates DBT in two ways. First it is a philosophy of "the fundamental nature of reality" (Linehan, 2015a, p. 4). Linehan points out how "dialectics expresses the fundamental interrelatedness or wholeness of reality." Looking only at the individual parts of a system overlooks how the parts affect each other. Linehan states, "Everything and every person is connected in some way" (Linehan, 2015b, p. 287). Seeing others as separate entities is one extreme, overlooking the other pole: we are also connected and are continuously affecting each other.

Here is one example to explain this dialectical way of looking at the world. In 1970, the Cincinnati Reds won 70 of their first 100 games and went to the World Series, but the following year they went downhill and only a won half their games. General Manager Bob Houseman engineered a blockbuster trade with the Houston Astros, swapping three players for five. One of the players coming to the Reds was second baseman Joe Morgan. Before the trade, Joe Morgan had been an above-average Major League baseball player. The Reds acquired him because they needed a speedy player who could steal a base.

When Morgan came to the Reds, manager Sparky Anderson deliberately assigned his locker next to Pete Rose's locker (Morgan and Falkner, 1993). Rose was known as "Charlie Hustle." He had won several batting titles and was a fierce competitor whose love of the game bordered on fanaticism. Joe Morgan stated that putting his locker next to Rose's was crucial in him becoming a better player. Rubbing elbows with Pete Rose taught him more about the game of baseball and the importance of hustle. Morgan went from being an above-average player to being a superstar. He became the catalyst for the Reds to go to the World Series three times in the next five years, winning back-to-back World Championships in 1975 and 1976. Joe Morgan was also voted the National League's Most Valuable Player in 1975.

The relationship between Joe Morgan, Pete Rose, and the rest of the Cincinnati Reds can only be understood by using dialectics. Without Rose, Morgan said he would have never become the superstar that he did. However, the player that Morgan became was uniquely him. Whoever had the locker next to Rose before 1972 didn't turn into the mega-star and dynamo that was Joe Morgan in a Cincinnati Reds uniform. Was Morgan the cause of this success? Or was it the new environment he found himself in? The dialectical answer is "both." To take either of these polarities out of the equation does an injustice to reality.

QUESTION: WHY DO OUR MINDS THINK NON-DIALECTICALLY?

If thinking dialectically is such a great thing, why is it that we often think in non-dialectical terms? Good question.

I believe there are several answers to this. First, the world is a complex place, but the evolution of our brains is still trying to catch up to that complexity. The ability to comprehend the complexities of physics, the biological sciences, and chemistry is usually only attained by a few of the brightest in our tribe, and even that only with great and sustained effort, A second reason is that thinking non-dialectically has served a very important purpose: sometimes there is an advantage to seeing the world in very simple, black and white, good and bad terms. For example, look at our reaction to snakes. Humans universally react with startle and fear to snakes. Typically, we jump away when we see one. The first time I stumbled upon a snake in a state park, I screamed and ran in sheer terror. This was a very adaptive response from an evolutionary point of view. Some snakes are poisonous, some are not. When in doubt, it is better to err on the side of safety. The instant perception that "snakes are bad!" is a helpful one.

But the idea that "snakes are bad" is not entirely true, and not entirely useful. Snakes play an important role in the eco-system, helping to keep it in balance. Snakes eat creatures we would rather not have around, such as insects and rodents. Many snakes do not put us in danger, and some people like having them as pets.

Sometimes, making snap judgments—"this is good, that is bad"—can be useful and helpful. But taking the categories of 'good" and "bad" literally is overly simplistic, and not useful apart from getting little boys to run away from snakes when they don't know whether or not are poisonous.

POLARIZED: THE SAD DOWNFALL OF A SUCCESSFUL EVANGELIST

Dialectics assume that the universe is full of contradictions. We look at one chunk of reality and label it thesis, and yet another part of reality as antitheses; our task is to work with the thesis and antithesis to come up with a more complex synthesis of the two. In Buddhism, this synthesis is called "the Middle Path" between two extremes. Marsha Linehan points out how much of what we call "psychopathology" is an individual getting "stuck in polarities, unable to move to synthesis" (1993, p. 35).

In the early 1980s, a friend of mine told me about a TV evangelist who played great piano and sang wonderful gospel music, so occasionally I would tune in and watch this evangelist on TV. In this story, I will simply call him "the Evangelist" He was probably the biggest Televangelist of the time, and those of you who are older may remember the series of events that I will describe. My point is not to shame this person, but rather to point out how often when people engage in actions they regret, it is not because they are insincere, and it may be because they had a dialectical breakdown.

I turned on the TV and watched the Evangelist. I loved his gospel music, but when he began preaching I was taken back. The Evangelist could be extremely strict, religiously perfectionistic, judgmental and punitive as he criticized young single Christian people about the sinfulness of having any physical contact with the opposite sex, even things like holding hands before marriage. He preached against having "lustful thoughts." Even in the days when I was much more religiously conservative (somewhat like the Evangelist himself), I thought he was going too far, going to an illogical extreme by advocating such strictness. The Evangelist warned his flock of falling into the devil's trap and losing their souls if they allowed themselves to have lustful thoughts. As such, I turned off the channel, not wanting to hear this polarized message, full of fire and brimstone.

Thinking about writing this, almost 40 years later, being a psychologist and knowing about the fallibility of human memory, I questioned myself: was The Evangelist as strict as I remembered? Doing research for this book, I read a well-critiqued biography of The Evangelist, which documented his strictness: he warned his listeners not to go to movies, even G-rated ones, because they might be exposed to previews for PG and R rated films (Seaman, 1999, p. 234). Seaman's book noted how his sermons and writings were "filled with diatribes against lust and warned against movies, dancing, masturbation, swimming, and even aerobics." (p. 343).

Several years later, the Evangelist was all over the news. He was caught frequenting prostitutes, and when caught by his church, he gave his famous, tearful "I have sinned" confession in public (it is on YouTube). Many people believed that The Evangelist was insincere, a hypocrite, and a con who played being a TV preacher because he was good at it and drew huge donations and fantastic sums of money. The research by the aforementioned author noted that in letters to the editor of major newspapers, readers thought he was a phony by a five to one margin (Seaman, 1999, p. 342), They believed that he had no intention of ever living the life he demanded of others.

I, however, never believed for a minute that the Evangelist was insincere or a fake. I saw him as a man caught in dialectical failure, going to one extreme and endorsing one polarity while invalidating the other. I believed the Evangelist was sincere, but had a dialectical breakdown.

It is true that traditional Christian teaching asserts that persons should not be mindlessly "ruled by the lust of the flesh." But at the same time, it is absurd to believe that the biologically based sexual urges in our body are "bad." If we did not have sexual urges, we would never have sex, and humanity would die out in a single generation. One has to experience hunger before being motivated to eat, thirst before one drinks. Chastising someone for being thirsty serves no good purpose. To believe it is wrong to have sexual desires and fantasies before marriage makes no sense. Thinking that something is intrinsically evil, then after marriage it suddenly and magically becomes "good," is a very polarized idea. If it were not for premarital "lust," nobody would be interested in getting married in the first place.

Marsha Linehan points out that non-dialectical thinking leads to "tendencies to think rigidly, and in absolute and extreme terms" (1993, p. 366). The dialectical behavior therapist helps the client "expand her cognitive options" beyond narrow, polarized categories. The Evangelist was shackled by his narrow thinking. He stated that the fields of psychology and counseling were of the devil, and advised his listeners to steer clear of them. The Evangelist even decried 12 Step groups (like Alcoholics Anonymous) for addictions and Christian counselors (Seaman, 1999, pp. 315, 333, 371). How unfortunate that he was not open to getting help for himself.

While I have no doubt that the Evangelist was sincere, I do believe that his absolute, all or nothing approach to trying to control urges set him up for failure (he was caught frequenting a prostitute again four years later). Though at one point he did take responsibility for his behavior (his famous "I have sinned" speech), at other junctures he blamed the devil, going so far as to claim the devil had taken control of him, as if he were on autopilot. He did not allow himself to deal with the other side of the polarity, the antithesis. Most of us want to do what is healthy, honorable and fair for all involved. But we also have the other side, the antithesis that wants to do just the opposite. The Evangelist's biographer refers to this as his "unfinished, dishonored part of himself" (Seaman, 1999, p. 289).

Note that I am not saying the Evangelist should have just acted out his antithesis (which is what he did). I believe this is similar to an example that Marsha Linehan gives, "at times you need to both control AND tolerate your emotions" (Linehan, 2015a, p. 152). At times, we need to both control our urges *and* tolerate them—yes, even have compassion toward the urges (and ourselves).

When we do not give the antithesis a voice in the dialog with thesis, antithesis will rebel, go rogue, and incite a behavioral insurrection. I witnessed this in my own religious background. A very kind, gentle, and ingratiating man was the manager of a church camp. He struck me as the kindest man I had ever met. One day, the old dining hall of the camp burned to the ground. The insurance adjuster investigating noted that a vehicle was also reported stolen about a year before.

When the hundred acres of the camp was searched, they found the lost vehicle was torched, then hidden in the woods. The investigation suggested that the kind and meek camp manager had torched both the car and the dining hall. Subsequent psychological treatment uncovered that he did so in an amnesic state.

Even if we choose to be kind and gentle, there is a side of us that sometimes gets angry, and needs to express ourselves. Pretending the other side of the polarity does not exist is not a viable solution. Pretending one side of the polarity isn't valid is not a stable foundation for building a life worth living.

A dialectical approach invites all parties to the negotiation table for dialogue.

POSITIVE PSYCHOLOGY IS DIALECTICAL: EVERYTHING IS NOT AWESOME

Positive psychology is the study of what can go right in human behavior, relationships, and emotional life. But positive psychology is not a philosophy that everything is "rainbows and unicorns," as portrayed in *The Lego Movie* (Lord & Miller, 2014) by the song, "Everything is Awesome." This tune was created to brainwash and oppress the citizens of Brickville into mindlessly following the dictates of their leader. At the end of the film, we discover who is pushing this anti-dialectical viewpoint, and how the purpose was to convince the citizens of this Lego world to ignore unpleasant emotions that would tell the citizens they want something different than the agenda of this leader. The end of the film reveals how one person was discounting the feelings of the other, and thus damaging their relationship. Don't let the very funny nature of this animated film fool you, it contains some deep themes that illustrate the importance of keeping relationships dialectical. In a healthy relationship, two people can have divergent—even contradictory—wishes (as in this film), but both can be valid, and both should be respected for the health of the relationship.

Positive psychology embraces both poles of a dialectical continuum, even noting the need to balance a positive mindset (optimism) with the negative one (pessimism).

As Seligman acknowledged in 1990, one must be careful not to be a "slave to the tyrannies of optimism," but be able to use pessimism keen sense of reality when we need it ... this insight has since been born out in empirical work, which reveals a diversity of problems associated with undue optimism, many related to under-appreciation of risk and subsequent maladaptive risk-taking.

(Ivtzan et al., 2016, p. 9)

Ivtzan and colleagues share examples of when a "positive" concept such as forgiveness can be negative, such as when an abuse victim forgives the abuser, which leads to being abused again. They point to the need to understand all factors in the person's environmental context. A scene in the movie *Gone with the Wind* depicts a similar situation: at a barbecue in Georgia, news breaks that the Civil War has commenced, and a number of enthusiastic, even jubilant southern men rush to enlist. Rhett Butler is confronted for not being enthusiastic, and he replies there is not a single cannon factory in the South. As Peterson (2006, p. 16) notes, positive psychology does not encourage persons to underestimate risks.

Linehan (2015b, p. 286) points out that for everything that exists, there is an opposite, and that it is impossible to understand any phenomenon without knowing it's opposite. Thus Ivtzan et al. point out that it is possible to love and hate a person at the same time, something that any experienced therapist knows and helps clients to understand. Likewise, for a person to have hope, there needs to be at least a notion of doubt and fear that things could turn out badly, otherwise hope would not be hope. They note that thought Positive Psychology focuses on helping people flourish; it also emphasizes that life is "inherently dialectical" and that "the good life involves an inevitable dialectic between positive and negative aspects of living" (p. 19). Put in Lego terms, everything is *not* awesome.

Ivtzan et al. point out that a significant amount of human growth comes when a person is the victim of negative, "bad" events, terming this "post-traumatic growth." They note "the dark times that we will encounter can also provide us with the possibility of learning from our struggles to become psychologically stronger and grow as humans" (p. 76). Struggling with the dark side of life is the catalyst for developing increased empathy for others, pushing us to appreciate the complexity of what they have had to wrestle with. Struggling with the negative aspects of life pushes us to reorganize our priorities, moving more spiritual and meaningful values to the front of the agenda. As a wise substance abuse counselor once told me, "our mistakes are our teachers."

Optimism and pessimism are both important, and both need to be held in dialectical balance. They are two different ways of looking at the world, and both contain elements of truth—neither should be discarded. Again, put in Lego terms, everything is NOT awesome. Thank God for this truth.

REFERENCES

Blatt, S J. (2008) *Polarities of experience: Relatedness and self-definition in personality development, psychopathology, and the therapeutic process.* Washington, DC, US: American Psychological Association. doi: 10.1037/11749-000.

Briere, J N. (1992) *Child abuse trauma: Theory and treatment of the lasting effects.* Newbury Park: Sage Productions.

Cash, J. (1997) *Cash: The autobiography.* New York: HarperCollins Publishers.

Forman, M (director). (1999) *Man on the Moon* [motion picture]. Universal Pictures.

Gartner, J (director). (2006) *Glory Road* [motion picture]. Walt Disney Pictures.

Haskins, D & Wetzel, D. (2006) *Glory Road: My story of the 1966 NCAA Basketball Championship and how one team triumphed against the odds and changed America forever.* New York: Hachette.

Ivtzan, I, Lomas, T, Hefferon, K, & Worth, P. (2016) *Second wave positive psychology. Embracing the dark side of life.* New York: Routledge.

Linehan, M M. (1993) *Cognitive-behavioral treatment of borderline personality disorder.* New York, NY, US: Guilford Press.

Linehan, M M. (2015a) *DBT skills training handouts and worksheets,* Second Edition. New York: Guilford Press.

Linehan, M M. (2015b) *DBT skills training manual.* New York: Guilford.

Lord, P & Miller, C (directors). (2014) *The Lego Movie.* Warner Brothers Pictures.

Lynch, T R. (2018a) *Radically open dialectical behavioral therapy: Theory and practice for treating disorders of overcontrol.* Oakland, CA, US: Context Press/New Harbinger Publications.

Lynch, T R. (2018b) *The Skills training manual for radically open dialectical behavioral therapy: A clinicians guide for treating disorders of overcontrol.* Oakland, CA, US: Context Press/New Harbinger Publications.

Mann, D. (2010) *Gestalt therapy: 100 key points & techniques.* New York: Routledge.

Mellencamp, J. (2010) *Save Some Time* [song], on *Better No than This.* Rounder Records.

Morgan, J & Falkner, D. (1993) *Joe Morgan: A life in baseball.* New York: W.W. Norton & Company.

Peterson, C. (2006) *A primer in positive psychology.* New York: Oxford University Press.

Peterson, J B. (1999) *Maps of meaning: The architecture of belief.* New York: Routledge.

Seaman, A. (1999) *Swaggart: The unauthorized biography of an American evangelist.* New York: Continuum.

Simon, P. (1964) *The Sound of Silence.* Universal Music Publishing.

Tirch, D, Silberstein, L R, & Kolts, R L. (2016) *Buddhist psychology and cognitive-behavioral therapy: A clinician's guide.* New York: Guilford Press.

Index